From Kokopellis to Electric Warriors

The Native American Culture of Music

By

Sandra Hale Schulman

© 2002 by Sandra Hale Schulman. All rights reserved.

No part of this book may be reproduced, stored in a retrieval system, or transmitted by any means, electronic, mechanical, photocopying, recording, or otherwise, without written permission from the author.

ISBN: 1-4033-4768-9 (e-book)
ISBN: 1-4033-4769-7 (Paperback)
ISBN: 1-4033-4770-0 (Dustjacket)

This book is printed on acid free paper.

1stBooks - rev. 07/11/02

With all my love to Mom for the roots and Dad for the wings

Special thanks to John Dolen, my first, best, and most generous editor

And to Ellen Bello for her endless vision and bottomless heart

Thanks also to my fellow hacks who make me want to be a better writer: Chet Flippo, Sean Piccoli, Melinda Newman, Deborah Evans-Price and Michael McCall

Table of Contents

1. Modern Traditionalists 1
2. The Storytellers 27
3. The Instrumentalists 43
4. Themes and Visions 57
5. Native Rock On A Roll 68
6. Indian / Country 101
7. Nashville's Trail of Hope October 10, 1998 116
8. Into The Mainstream: NAMA 129
9. The Festivals 165
10. Mr. Las Vegas: Wayne Newton 175
11. A Journey Home Along The Tourist Trap Trail 185

From Kokopellis to Electric Warriors
The Native American Culture of Music

Chapter One

Modern Traditionalists

Let's start with the basics. In it's simplest terms, Native American Music can be categorized by:

* Instrumentation
* Lyrical content
* Cadence of native languages spoken

Traditional lyrics & instrumentation include:

* Family songs
* Tribal ritual songs
* Powwow drum
* Rattle
* Flute

Contemporary lyrics & instrumentation are:

* Themes of great loss
* Endurance in the face of adversity
* Celebration of the on-going spirit of Native Americans
* Synthesizer
* Electric and bass guitar

The earliest known inhabitants of North America were a highly music-and-dance-oriented people who responded to their environment by creating a vast repertoire of unwritten songs and dances long before the arrival of the Europeans. The most well known petroglyph, a primitive rock carving, in the Southwest is that of a Kokopelli, a mystical little flute player who is known as a harbinger of good luck and fertility. These songs and dances were transmitted orally from generation to generation down to the present day. The descendants of those early tribal musicians continue to create and perform their unique art in the many ceremonials and rituals as well as public fairs and powwows that take place annually throughout the continental United States, Canada, and Alaska. Although many Native Americans have been assimilated into modern society, most tribal groups are making serious efforts to preserve their traditional cultures.

From the end of the Civil War to 1890, the year of the Wounded Knee massacre, the temper of the times discouraged sympathetic understanding or wide dissemination of Indian music and dance beyond tribal circles. Since then, however, frequent cross-cultural contacts between Indians and non-Indians, aided by modern travel and communications, have exerted a definite influence on the older forms of tribal music and dance. Nevertheless, each regional and geographic cultural area has fiercely retained its own identity just as, in most instances, the identity of each tribe has been tenaciously retained. If a song or dance is "borrowed," it is immediately suspected or recognized by the tribal music masters as coming from a specific cultural area, such as the Eastern Woodlands territory, the Great Plains, the Southwest, California and the Pacific Northwest, the Great Basin and Plateau, or Alaska and the Arctic Circle.

The music of the North American Indians is primarily vocal-monodic (single melodic line). All songs, both melody and words, have been and continue to be composed by individuals and "head singers," either male or female. Some songs are conceived during visionary or dreamlike states, while others are consciously created for special functions.

Some Indian music is strongly rhythmic, some predominantly melodic, sometimes whole words are sung, sometimes only syllables. Likewise, some dances are energetic and agitated, while others are placid and sedate. Occasionally, music and dancing are used merely for personal exposure in a public performance before an invited audience. Nearly always, however, dance is accompanied by vocal music and some kind of percussive instruments.

Accompaniment is mainly percussive: drums with animal-skin heads and rattles, shakers, and scrapers made of various materials such as deer hooves, seashells, bird beaks or animal horns. Flutes, whistles, and some stringed instruments are also used. All music is functional and accompanies specific activities such as dance, work, games, prayer, harvesting, healing, hunting, whaling, burial ceremonies, etc. Chants may contain many vocals or nontranslatable vocal sounds and may have either elaborate or simple language and narrative content.

Many attempts have been made to codify the formal structures of Indian songs, which appear to be rigidly composed within the context of their respective functions. For example, the war dance songs of the Plains Indians generally have a descending contour with an introduction followed by variations of A—as in the formula AA' BA' CA'—ending with a "tail-dance" section that reiterates part of the principal section. These seemingly simple chants are so varied, however, that it is virtually impossible to isolate hard and fast rules for their composition due to language differences among the various tribal cultures, the differences in stylistic coloration among the individual singers, and the regionalism and variety of dance styles.

While traditional forms of tribal music retain their melodic and historical links with the past through oral transmission, the increasing availability of sound recordings and the documentation of Indian chants has increased the musical skills and expanded the repertoire of the tribal songmakers. Moreover, in Missouri, Colorado, Arkansas, and other border areas, there are non-Indian folklorists who perform Indian dances and songs in the Indian style. Also, far afield, in Europe (Germany, France, Finland) there are non-Indian clubs of American Indian wannabes who present their folklore programs with full regalia.

Other forms of North American Indian music familiar to the public through the concert hall, the cinema, and popular music are often, at best, quasi-romantic, pseudoethnic versions of Western music that have never reflected the true spirit of Indian music. Antonin Dvorak's prophecy that America should have a national music based on North American Indian songs will be fulfilled only when our creative artists scalp the old cliches and seek more valid art forms inspired by an understanding and love of Indian music. A dramatic example of this is Walela's Cherokee language version of Amazing Grace, but more on them later.

North American Indian music has undergone a transmutation of values in the oral-to-written process, the results of which have been intended for non-Indian audiences; tribal music has remained in its original state only where the Indians have remained on the fringes of American society. This won't always be the case, however, as this music comes to be understood and felt deeply by an ever-growing audience, and music industry, receptive to its unique artistic value. The use of Indian elements in today's performing arts can be a revitalizing factor in American music and music education.

An excellent example of a successful ensemble is award winning Robert Mirabal and his band Tribal Mob, who have toured to wide acclaim with a highly theatrical show that fuses the roots of his Taos Pueblo home with rock and folk music, along with dance, instruments from all over the world and outrageous costumes. Mirabal's show has been aired for over a year on public television stations.

From Kokopellis to Electric Warriors
The Native American Culture of Music

Another group, the E-Yah-Pah-Hah Indian Chanters, was a development of the first bicultural music education program of the Bureau of Indian Affairs. It featured Indian songs, poetry, and mime within the framework of a modern choir. Also, the initial performance of the first all-Indian half-time marching band at an American football game took place at RFK Stadium in Washington, D.C., in 1977; and 150 young Indian musicians from 80 tribes and 30 states performed a pageant called "American Indian Heroes, History and Heritage." Carlos Nakai performs with top jazz musicians, creating a unearthly hybrid of ancient flute and 1950s smoky guitar.

Many of the current Native American musicians owe a great deal to their heritage, and rather than experiment with new forms of musical hybrids, they prefer to revive and preserve original forms of the music of their tribal heritages. The old is now being heralded by the young as something new.

Joanne Shenandoah

Great critical acclaim has been heaped on singer, songwriter, performer, and composer Joanne Shenandoah of the Oneida Six

Nations Iroquois. This sweet and prolific songbird opened Woodstock 1994 with her moving song America, she has also performed at the White House, on The Nashville Network, and the TV show Northern Exposure, Earth Day on the Mall, the Special Olympics, various music festivals and state fairs across the nation including both of President Clinton's inaugurations and a private performance for First Lady Hillary Clinton and Mrs. Tipper Gore.

Shenandoah has created sound tracks for numerous television shows and video documentaries. She tours with many country artists as well as with her sister to shows at reservations and she claims that three women are always on stage with her "in spirit."

"Shenandoah has become the most critically acclaimed Native American singer of her time" - Associated Press.

A few of Shenandoah's laurels include:

* NAIRD's - Native American Record of the Year INDIE Award 1997

* Native American Woman of Hope - 1997

* Outstanding Achievement Award - 1997, Syracuse NewsPapers

* Native American Woman's Recognition Award - 1996

* Outstanding Musical Achievement nominee for 1995 & 1996, Awardee 1994.

* Female Artist of the Year 1999 - Native American Music Awards

Shenandoah is a Wolf Clan member of the Iroquois Confederacy - Oneida Nation. Her original compositions, combined with her striking voice, enables her to embellish the ancient songs of the Iroquois using a blend of traditional and contemporary instrumentation. Ms. Shenandoah's music reflects the indigenous philosophy and culture which continues to have a profound effect on the world today.

From traditional chants to contemporary ballads about Native ways, her music has been described as an emotional experience, a "Native American Trance".

"...She weaves you into a trance with her beautiful Iroquois chants and wraps her voice around you like a warm blanket on a cool winter's night."—Robbie Robertson

Sandra Hale Schulman

She is the author of Skywoman, which includes Legends of the Iroquois with co-writer Doug George. Shenandoah also appears on Robbie Robertson's CD Contact from the Underworld of Redboy.

Hapa

Out in the middle of the Pacific Ocean, musical traditions are being kept alive by Hapa, Hawaiian music makers who play Slack-Key - a personal and distinctly native Hawaiian form of family music passed down over the decades but never recorded. Slack Key was thought to have originated about a century and a half ago when Westerners brought guitars to the islands. When they left, the untuned guitars were left behind with the keys loosened or slacked. While the untuned style led to odd picking and strumming sounds, Hawaiians refer to it as heart music, a sort of native blues that's slow and soothing, a gentle swing like the Pacific surf.

But over time this deeply felt Slack Key music had been withering due to it's public obscurity and mainland influences like rock and roll.

"I'm old enough to remember the time when we thought it would actually die," says Hawaiian composer Keola Beamer. "because part of the mystique of the slack key guitar was the reluctance of the players to share information. I think that the Hawaiians had so much taken away from them - their land, their religious systems, everything - the only thing left was the music."

Guitarists even hid the secrets of slack-key tunings and playing from each other.

"Each family had their own style of tuning and used to kind of hide it away and keep it behind doors, so the only time they'd play was at special parties" recalls a Hawaiian musician who grew up in the 1950s. "When I was a boy of about nine, I was at a luau. Underneath a mango tree I heard this beautiful slack key guitar. I ran up to the guy, sat at his feet and looked right at him. He took a good look at me, stopped playing and faced the other way. I wasn't a member of his family. The irony of it was that because people were holding this thing so close it was dying. The music only began to open up during the war."

Sandra Hale Schulman

The first slack key guitar album was released in 1960 by Leonard Kwan. Beamer wrote a book in 1973 on the various tunings and the first public concerts took place in 1972, when it became part of a larger Hawaiian cultural preservation movement. Hapa's (Hapa means half in Hawaiian) interpretation and revival of the form has made them the best known new Hawaiian group since Don Ho.

Hapa is Barry Flanagan (an Irishman from the States) and Keli'l Kaneali'l (a native Hawaiian). Their debut self titled album features musicians Stephen Stills from the American folk group Crosby, Stills & Nash; and Kenny Loggins of Loggins & Messina.

Hapa's debut became the fastest selling record in Hawaiian history, selling hundreds of thousands of albums and capturing all the top music awards given in that state. The album carries both the English and Hawaiian language translations, portions of the sale proceeds go toward Maui's Hawaiian Language Immersion Pre-School - Punana Leo O Maui. The school teaches the native language to Maui's school children. The album has distribution in the U.S. and is published by a World music record label in Florida.

From Kokopellis to Electric Warriors
The Native American Culture of Music

Rita Coolidge and Walela

One of the entertainment world's great beauties and great success stories is Cherokee Rita Coolidge. The daughter of a Nashville preacher, Rita Coolidge sang in church choirs growing up, the result of being the daughter of a Southern Preacher but it wasn't all that tough, she has said.

"It wasn't as strict as you'd imagine while I was growing up," says Coolidge. "Back in the '60s when the Beatles came to the South, the Baptist Association told everyone to burn all their records. It was crazy. But my father told me to go and enjoy the concert and forget what everyone was doing. He may be a preacher but he's always given me a lot of freedom to make my own decisions and mistakes… and there have been many along the way."

Rita and her sister Priscilla grew up in the South in a family of four children and a strong Native American Heritage. Their dad a Baptist minister, their mom a school teacher who gave music lessons and played organ in the church. The Coolidge home was filled with the sounds that ignited their musical imagination and enlightened their spirit to soar into creation.

While attending Florida State University, she fronted her own group, R.C. and the Moonpies. She signed with jazz visionary Herb Alpert's label, and her 1971 self-titled album was an immediate bestseller. Rita charted Top 10 Hits "Higher and Higher" and "We're All Alone," and has collaborated with Kris Kristofferson (to whom she was married and has a daughter), Eric Clapton, Robbie Robertson and many more.

Coolidge has proven herself with an enduring talent blessed with radiant Native American beauty and what has been described as "the sexiest voice in the world."

A two time Grammy winner, her recording career has spawned over several dozen albums worldwide including her multi-platinum disc "Anytime... Anywhere" which featured three of her biggest hit singles—"Higher & Higher," "The Way You Do The Things You Do," and "We're All Alone."

Rita's commitment to social issues has consistently reverberated through her music and her life on such issues as teen suicide, AIDS and homelessness.

From Kokopellis to Electric Warriors
The Native American Culture of Music

"What I do is my life and what I am. Being able to sing is a very special thing to have, and I really feel like a very lucky person to be able to do what I do. I love it."

Her most heartfelt commitment remains to the Native American community and has been heard throughout the soundtrack of the HBO movie Grand Avenue and seen co-hosting the 1997 First Americans In The Arts Awards.

The commitment to her Cherokee heritage carries through her life, "If we have the vision and the dream, anything can come true," she says.

With a high profile career that has spanned three decades, Coolidge decided to bring it all back home to her roots. Forming a group with her sister Priscilla and her niece Laura Satterfield, the trio call themselves Walela, the Cherokee word for Hummingbird and the symbol of inspiration for this family of women singers.

The music on Walela's debut album is intensely spiritual and ethereal, a soaring, rhythmic and melodic harmony of three blood relatives that intertwines Native American and Southern music traditions.

Sandra Hale Schulman

Priscilla Coolidge, who for two years running was voted the best female vocalist by Billboard Magazine, has carved out a deep niche in modern music. She has recorded with a who's who of music including Bob Dylan, Luther Vandross, Robbie Robertson and has penned tunes recorded by her sister Rita, Willie Nelson, Emmylou Harris, and Maurice White of Earth, Wind and Fire.

Never one to compromise, Priscilla recorded for A&M and Capricorn Records the music that reflected the deep spiritual nature of herself and her father, a minister of full-blooded Cherokee descent.

Laura Satterfield, born into this glamorous musical family, grew up listening to the many talents that surrounded her. Having fallen in love with their spirit, she began her own journey of musical discovery. In the tradition that came before her, Laura has made her own place in the recording industry. Well known for her angelic looks and spirited writing abilities, Laura has found her own style which can be heard in the movie Made In America where she performs her creation "I Don't Walk on Water." She also released a solo album in 2000 called Dirty Velvet Lie. Robbie Robertson has described Satterfield as "one in five million, a true gift and blessing."

From Kokopellis to Electric Warriors
The Native American Culture of Music

Here's what music industry bible Billboard wrote about Walela's first album:

(June 21, 1997) Billboard WALELA turns to its roots on Triloka Debut by Steve Mirkin (LOS ANGELES)

World music has carved out a comfortable niche for itself in the marketplace by highlighting various musics from all over the globe, but will U.S. fans of the genre take an interest in the music of American Indians?

With the July 24th self titles album by Walela, a vocal trio featuring Rita Coolidge, Triloka Records will see if this is the case. Mitchell Markus, Triloka's president, thinks the time is right for American Indian music to receive a bigger audience. He backs up his assertions by referring to the sales of Robbie Robertson & the Red Road Ensemble's "Music for the Native Americans" album, as well as ratings of such documentaries as PBS' "The West," which Markus says reflects an interest in American Indian history and culture.

Sandra Hale Schulman

Markus also points out that the Sante Fe, N.M.-based label, which is marketed and distributed through Mercury, has had some success with its previous American Indian releases, such as the multi-artist "Songs of the Spirit." Walela's prospects for crossover success are improved, however, by Coolidge's name recognition among mainstream consumers. Coolidge, best known for her 1977 cover of "Higher And Higher," is half-Cherokee and describes her participation in Walela in mystical terms.

"This is an album for the heavens," she says, adding that she is especially pleased to be working with her sister Priscilla Coolidge (an accomplished singer/songwriter who has performed with Bob Dylan and written songs for Wille Nelson and Emmylou Harris) and with her niece Laura Satterfield.

The trio first appeared on Robertson's "Native Americans" album on which they performed "Cherokee Morning Song" (which they reprise on "Walela"). The Coolidges and Satterfield were so taken with the results that they began to perform as Walela (Cherokee for "hummingbird").

*From Kokopellis to Electric Warriors
The Native American Culture of Music*

Triloka's Markus heard them play in Sante Fe and saw the crossover potential. "Walela," he says, is a unique mix of songs reflecting American Indian concerns, the music encompassing the Coolidges' upbringing by a Baptist minister father of Cherokee descent and a music-teaching mother of Scottish descent. The result is a mixture of ethereal voice floating above music that has elements of gospel, new-age, and folk; the blend is heard to best effect on the groups version of "Amazing Grace." The hymn is translated into Cherokee and arranged with bagpipes wailing in the background.

Rita Coolidge, who feels that too many American Indian albums get pigeonholed into the new-age category, says that Walela wants to be "regarded as indigenous music"; Markus calls the act's music "contemporary Native American." David Silver; VP of A&R at Mercury, who oversees Triloka's releases, thinks that Walela "is perfect for Triloka." Mercury, he says, will be able to give the album a profile in the mainstream market - which includes, in addition to radio and retail, a presence in the international market and a chance to do soundtrack work. Markus and Silver agree that before any of the above can take place, Walela has to perform well in the American

Sandra Hale Schulman

Indian market. "You have to saturate your base before you cross over," Silver says. The label has hired Soar; a firm that specializes in marketing to American Indians, to maximize its efforts. Most American Indian albums, Markus explains, fall into either the "powwow" or new-age categories, but Markus does not think the polyglot nature of Walela's music will be a problem.

"The market is so diffuse," he says, citing tribal and language differences. Soar will help place the album into such non-traditional outlets as trading posts, reservation gift shops, and new age bookstores. Walela has already started to attract attention in the American Indian community. Triloka sent advance copies to American Indian publications and reservation newspapers, and the response, he says, has been universally positive.

"This is the album that Rita's contemporaries have been waiting for her to make," he says. "the approval of the Native Americans is also important to the Coolidges."

Rita Coolidge says, "A lot of Native American culture gets lost... It's very important that Native Americans hear this album."

*From Kokopellis to Electric Warriors
The Native American Culture of Music*

Since many of the targeted outlets fall outside of the traditional music retail community, sales are very hard to gauge, and Silver has to rely more on instinct and orders in deciding when to make his move into the mainstream.

In the meantime he had been laying the groundwork for the group at Mercury.

"Part of my job," Silver says, "is to make sure that when it is time for Walela to crossover, we are ready."

Copies of the album will be serviced to triple-A radio, with Satterfield's solo showcase, "The Warrior," expected to be the emphasis track TV will also play a part in the promotional campaign. Walela appeared on "Late Show with David Letterman" along with Robertson two years ago, and Markus expects the act to be booked as a solo act. In addition, he says, shows like "Good Morning America" and "Regis and Kathi Lee" have expressed an interest in the group. But more important to Walela is its appearance July 24 at the opening ceremonies for the Smithsonian Institution's Native American Museum, which will be followed by a tour that will find the act performing at Nature Company outlets and Borders bookstores.

Sandra Hale Schulman

As a group, Walela continues to disperse the energy and spirit which has brought them to this juncture in their lives. Featured as part of Robbie Robertson's Red Road Ensemble album "Music for Native Americans," their distinctive vocal blend brings to life "The Cherokee Morning Song" and has allowed them to tour to an international audience. During the 1996 Atlanta Olympics, Walela represented their nations—both Cherokee and the United States—as they performed in the Olympic Park. They also performed at the 2002 Winter Olympics Opening Ceremony in Salt Lake City, Utah for an audience estimated at 2 billion.

Walela won awards and performed at the First Native American Music Awards Show and showed up to present and lend support at the second show despite Laura's bad head cold. They made quite a stunning group, with Rita and Priscilla's gleaming jet black hair, heavy velvet skirts and large one of a kind jewelry pieces. Satterfield has the looks of an angel, with a halo of white blond hair and slinky West coast style. Smiling, laughing and gracious to the ultimate degree, the Coolidge sisters epitomize the spirit of Native American performers.

The year 2000 found Walela continuing to tour in support of their second album "Unbearable Love". This album delves further into gospel music as interpreted by the group, with standout songs "I Know I Don't Walk On Water" and "Smoke In The Wind".

Sandra Hale Schulman

Joanne Shenandoah and sister at Micosukee Fest, 12/96 (above and below)

From Kokopellis to Electric Warriors
The Native American Culture of Music

HAPA

Sandra Hale Schulman

Walela
Photo – Stephen Shadrach

Chapter Two

The Storytellers

Stories of the past, along with legends that contain morals and lessons are a major part of Native American history. This is the way cultures have been handed down, by telling and retelling, from older family members to younger ones. So much of the recorded history has been lost, as languages disappear and stories fly away like leaves in the wind.

But in this new age, Indians are making up for the loss. There are new ways of communication - books, videos, film, the internet and compact discs now carry the messages and become the storytellers.

"We are more than just writers. We are [Native] storytellers. We are spokespeople. We are cultural ambassadors. We are politicians. We are activists. We are all of this simply by nature of what we do, without even wanting to be."—Sherman Alexie

Sandra Hale Schulman

Sherman J. Alexie, Jr. was born in October 1966. He is a Spokane/Coeur d'Alene Indian (he prefers to be called an Indian, finding Native American a "guilty white liberal term") and was born and raised in the Spokane Indian Reservation in Wellpinit, Washington, about 50 miles from Spokane.

His father held various jobs, including truck driver and logger and his mother was a social worker. Alexie was born hydrocephalic and underwent a brain operation at the age of 6 months, and was not expected to survive. When he did beat the odds, doctors predicted he would live with severe mental retardation. Although spared this, he suffered through seizures and other problems throughout his childhood. Preferring to stay inside (or occasionally hide in the rocks on the reservation), he developed an intense love for reading, reading Steinbeck as a five-year-old.

The following is an excerpt from an essay of Alexie's called "The Joy of Reading - Superman and Me" from April, 1998 and is included in a recent anthology published by Milkweed Editions, entitled "The Most Wonderful Books: Writers on Discovering the Pleasures of

From Kokopellis to Electric Warriors
The Native American Culture of Music

Reading." It is reprinted here with the kind permission of the publisher.

"I learned to read with a Superman comic book. Simple enough, I suppose. I cannot recall which particular Superman comic book I read, nor can I remember which villain he fought in that issue. I cannot remember the plot, nor the means by which I obtained the comic book. What I can remember is this: I was 3 years old, a Spokane Indian boy living with his family on the Spokane Indian Reservation in eastern Washington state. We were poor by most standards, but one of my parents usually managed to find some minimum-wage job or another, which made us middle-class by reservation standards. I had a brother and three sisters. We lived on a combination of irregular paychecks, hope, fear and government surplus food.

My father, who is one of the few Indians who went to Catholic school on purpose, was an avid reader of westerns, spy thrillers, murder mysteries, gangster epics, basketball player biographies and anything else he could find. He bought his books by the pound at

Dutch's Pawn Shop, Goodwill, Salvation Army and Value Village. When he had extra money, he bought new novels at supermarkets, convenience stores and hospital gift shops. Our house was filled with books. They were stacked in crazy piles in the bathroom, bedrooms and living room. In a fit of unemployment-inspired creative energy, my father built a set of bookshelves and soon filled them with a rare assortment of books about the Kennedy assassination, Watergate, the Vietnam War and the entire 23-book series of the Apache westerns. My father loved books, and since I loved my father with an aching devotion, I decided to love books as well.

I can remember picking up my father's books before I could read. The words themselves were mostly foreign, but I still remember the exact moment when I first understood, with a sudden clarity, the purpose of a paragraph. I didn't have the vocabulary to say "paragraph," but I realized that a paragraph was a fence that held words. The words inside a paragraph worked together for a common purpose. They had some specific reason for being inside the same fence. This knowledge delighted me. I began to think of everything in terms of paragraphs. Our reservation was a small paragraph within the

United States. My family's house was a paragraph, distinct from the other paragraphs of the LeBrets to the north, the Fords to our south and the Tribal School to the west. Inside our house, each family member existed as a separate paragraph but still had genetics and common experiences to link us. Now, using this logic, I can see my changed family as an essay of seven paragraphs: mother, father, older brother, the deceased sister, my younger twin sisters and our adopted little brother."

As a young adult, Alexie faced a new problem: alcoholism. Alcohol plagued his life for five years before he became sober at 23.

He attended high school at Reardan High where he was "the only Indian... except for the school mascot." Alexie graduated with honors and planned to be a doctor until he "fainted three times in human anatomy class and needed a career change." That change was fueled when Alexie stumbled into a poetry workshop at Washington State University in Pullman. He attended Gonzaga University in Spokane on a scholarship and graduated in American Studies from Washington State. Alexie received the Washington State Arts Commission Poetry

Sandra Hale Schulman

Fellowship in 1991 and the National Endowment for the Arts Poetry Fellowship in 1992.

Soon after receiving his second fellowship, he cranked out six poetry books and poem/short story books, including the award winners "The Business of Fancydancing" and "The Lone Ranger and Tonto Fistfight in Heaven."

This put the total number of pieces of work, including pieces written for magazines and anthologies, at over 300 poems, stories, essays and reviews. "I don't believe in writer's block," Alexie says. "Artists are essentially lazy and I'm not."

His first novel, "Reservation Blues," found him named one of Granta's Best of Young American Novelists and won him the Before Columbus Foundation's American Book Award and the Murray Morgan Prize. His second novel, "Indian Killer", was named one of People's Best of Pages and a New York Times Notable Book.

For a while, he did a combination reading/music tour with friend Jim Boyd, a Colville Indian. Alexie and Boyd also collaborated to record the album "Reservation Blues," which contains the songs from the book of the same name. The album won Best Soundtrack album at the 1999 NAMA Awards.

One of the Reservation Blues songs, "Small World," also appeared on "Talking Rain: Spoken Word & Music from the Pacific Northwest" and "Honor: A Benefit for the Honor the Earth Campaign."

Chris Eyre, a Cheyenne/Arapaho Indian, was a grad student at New York University's film school when he read some of Alexie's work. Through a mutual friend, they agreed to collaborate on a film project. The basis for the screenplay was "This is What it Means to Say Phoenix, Arizona," a short story from "The Lone Ranger and Tonto Fistfight in Heaven."

Released as "Smoke Signals" at the Sundance Film Festival, the movie won two awards. After the Sundance success, "Smoke Signals" found a distributor, Miramax Films, and was released in New York and Los Angeles in 1998.

The film was the first one to be written, directed and produced by Native Americans, but it showed the commonality of the breakdown of American family life, on reservations and in every city in the country. But Alexie also sees how that commonality has erased cultural identity.

"Most Indians probably can't even spell sovereignty," states Alexie, just one in a series of inflamatory comments he loves to drop.

Another of his efforts, "One Stick Song" is filled with even more. It's a collection of poems and thought provoking short stories that put Alexie back in his most comfortable element.

"I like poetry and short stories the best", Alexie told Indianz.Com. "It's also what I'm best at."

Although Alexie has stated many of his prior works are based on personal experiences, two stories in the collection, "The Unofficial Autobiography of Me" and "The Warriors" give readers an inside glimpse into Alexie that many may not have seen before. The stories offer tidbits of life many in Indian Country can relate to, such as going to a KISS concert, playing on the tribal baseball team, and growing up on the reservation.

"The Warriors" discusses an issue many are aware of but hardly talk about: an Indian person's attraction to someone of another race. In this case, it's Alexie's "secret" fascination with white women.

"I lusted after white girls and women more than I lusted after Indian girls and women," writes Alexie. "Television taught me to do this. Television taught me that the bodies of white women were more beautiful than the bodies of brown women."

Later, Alexie writes about falling in love with and marrying a Hidatsa / Ho-Chunk / Potawatomi woman who "has beautiful, clear, brown skin and long, raven-black hair."

"One Stick Song," like his other recent effort, "The Toughest Indian in The World," also inspires discussion about every day Indian life that not many others write about.

"60 percent of Indians are urban Indians and nobody's writing about them," says Alexie. "Everybody thinks the rez is Eden. Everybody thinks the rez is where you're the most Indian."

The stories in "One Stick Song" give readers a glimpse inside Sherman Alexie, a picture often masked by his public persona. But according to Alexie, we all wear masks in our lives.

"We all wear masks, says Alexie. "We're all liars."

So is Sherman Alexie lying, just joking, or both? The more you read of his the less telling he is. Even a writer as prolific as Alexie still feels that "I know I have so much left to say and I don't know how much time I have left to say it all."

In his personal life, Alexie has one child with his wife, Diane, a college counselor and Hidatsa Indian. She is also a former basketball player, like Alexie himself (a 6'2" shooting guard). They live in Seattle.

Russell Means

The Los Angeles Times has described Russell Means as the most famous American Indian since Sitting Bull and Crazy Horse. Russell Means is a natural leader. His fearless dedication and indestructible sense of pride are qualities admired by nations worldwide, but have also been an enormous source of controversy. He is outspoken, obstinate and unrepentant about his vision and views of indigenous people as he sees the need for people to be:

"Free to be human, free to travel, free to stop, free to trade where they choose, free to choose their own teachers, free to follow the religion of their fathers, free to talk, think and act for themselves and then they will obey every law or submit to the penalty. The most difficult lesson of all is to respect your relatives' visions," he says.

An early supporter of the AIM movement, Means has used the entertainment world as a massive platform for Indian rights. Acting in films (Last of the Mohicans, Buffalo Girls, Pocahontas, Natural Born Killers, Wind Runner, Wagons East) and recording protest albums with Tom Bee, Means has alienated some but enlightened many more as to the hardships and realities of modern Indian life.

On his album "Electric Warrior" (Soar 1993), he calls the music rap-ajo. It features a striking cover painting of Means by avant pop artist Andy Warhol. The songs range from less than a minute to more than eight minutes of poetry/chants layered over music that vibrates with strings, drums, synthesizers and natural sounds of water and lightening. Song titles resonate with uprisings and calls for change – "AIM IS Still Alive," "Nuclear World," "Seventh Generation," "Remember Wounded Knee" and "What Tribe Are You."

Means co-wrote an autobiography "Where White Men Fear To Tread" in the mid 1990's in which he demeans the modern Powwow:

Sandra Hale Schulman

"It is the songs, not the language, that have always been the most important part of our cultural heritage. We have songs for everything. They tell us where we came from and why, where we're going and why. Songs tell us everything we need to know to be a human being and a proud member of our nation."

"But because of intertribal powwows many Indian nations have all but lost the songs and dances that were unique to their nations. Starting in the 1950s city dwelling Indians can go to powwows where they can dress up for a few hours a month to play Indian as if that can justify their Indian blood. The rest of the time they are lost in the maze of white society. Since the powwows began the Indian nations have become weaker year by year. They have become caricatures of their own traditions, unrecognizable as communities, as nations, almost as Indians."

"Some people lament the loss of those old songs," Means continues "but Lakota Holy Man Fools Crow says most Indians don't deserve to retain them. You have to live a way of life that has value and principals and freedom - a responsible life governed by spirituality. Then you deserve your culture, including it's songs, and you deserve to know the secrets of your heritage.

The songs are about beauty and tradition and respect and love - all the good things our culture has enjoyed for eons. We dance for our ancestors, as long as the songs go on we are free Indians. Tourists know nothing of all that. They thinks it's quaint and primitive to chant and beat a tom tom. They never realize that the rhythm is the heartbeat of our nation, the pulse of our entire existence on earth - that our songs were handed down from one generation to another for centuries. Dancing for tourists, I came to know exactly how a prostitute feels when they sell their bodies. When my culture is violated, so is everything that I am".

While his own life has been marked by abuse, knock down drag out bar brawls and jail stays, he now thinks "The solution is understanding life and not fighting it. Accepting it and embracing it and living with peace of mind - that's what traditional Indians have."

But Means is nothing if not a modern day Indian. Forget smoke signals, he learned firsthand the power of the press. When news of the 1969 Indian occupation of Alcatraz island in San Francisco Bay hit

TV and newspapers, Means says he "was amazed by all the print and TV coverage. It was my first inkling of what direct action can accomplish through the media - and the authorities missed the point completely and treated our claim as though it were nothing more than a publicity stunt. Looking back I'm not surprised White America has always trivialized Indian people."

"We're not real human beings, we don't exist, we have no cars, no rights, no sensibilities. We're tourist attractions. To this very day, women come up to me and grab my braids. That's a violation of my person."

But after playing into white society in his early years and meeting nothing but frustration, he came to embrace Indian customs, language, dress and icons. He finds significance in natures colors: pink is medicinal power, blue is universe, black is thunderclouds and thunder spirits that equal cleanliness and purity. Red is energy, strength, endurance, yellow is morning, white is southern warm winds, brown the living races of all people. Purple is sunset, green is plant life. Four is a sacred number - four points of the universe, four winds, four directions, four ages of earth, four ages of humans, four seasons, four quarters of the moon.

These things are adopted by both conservative and radical Indians like the members of the American Indian Movement. When Means first saw their beaded belts, sashes, chokers, moccasins, headbands and Indian jewelry he thought "what are they trying to prove? Those guys looked ridiculous all dressed up like Indians."

But now that is how Means dresses, presenting to the world - and the media - the pride of his roots. While he still has the power to create a stir - his controversial appearance at the 1999 Native American Music Awards in Albuquerque was canceled after he made inflammatory remarks about an Indian/FBI murder trial - he still travels, lectures and acts as a storyteller in movies and his own life, with his own myth standing as tall as any of them.

Sandra Hale Schulman

Russell Means

Chapter Three

The Instrumentalists

The eerie sound of a flute, the spine tingling pound of a drum, the snaky hiss of a rattle - Native American music all starts with the instruments: drums with animal-skin heads and rattles, shakers, and scrapers made of various materials including deer hooves, seashells, bird beaks and animal horns.

This chapter explores some of the instruments used and tells the story of some of the more well known instrumentalists.

R. Carlos Nakai, flautist and author of the Art of the Native American Flute

To become the world's premier Native American flutist, R. Carlos Nakai had to rely more on research and innovation and less on his Navajo-Ute heritage. While his tribe the Diné had a strong flute-playing tradition, it was lost when they migrated from the Northwest Plains of Canada to the Southwest over five centuries ago.

While Nakai may not have been "born to the flute," it was curiosity about his heritage that led him to it. During the late 1960s while researching American Indian music and traditional instruments, the wooden flute piqued Nakai's interest, but it wasn't until 1972 that he took it up seriously. Prior to that Nakai had devoted his musical energies to classical training on the brass instruments cornet and trumpet.

In his dogged determination to have a thorough knowledge of the instrument, Nakai set out to craft his own. From a flute-making teacher he learned that rather than the oak Nakai was using, cedar is the only wood that works well. He also discovered that when it comes to flute making, there are no standard dimensions. The finger holes and air column are based on hand and finger measurements and are never the same. As a result, each flute has a different sound and pitch which makes the tonality of the instruments random. Nakai views each flute less as a musical instrument than "as a sound sculpture - a piece of art that also creates sound".

From Kokopellis to Electric Warriors
The Native American Culture of Music

Part of Nakai's philosophy is to ensure that the native flute does not become a "museum piece" or part of a bygone culture. Through his dynamic original compositions and other musical collaborations, Nakai shows the instrument's versatility and capabilities.

Over the past two decades, Nakai has melded his classical training with his expertise on the cedar flute to form a joyful, complex and sophisticated sound that not only reveals the flute's uniqueness, but covers the spectrum of musical genres: jazz ensembles, piano and guitar collaborations, and the concert hall.

In further experimentations, Nakai creates new sounds for the flute using electronic technology such as synthesizers and digital delay. A native Arizonan, Nakai's southwestern surroundings as well as his culture, heavily influence his work.

"A lot of what I've been taught culturally, comes from an awareness of the environment... How I feel is based on my impressions of being in certain spaces at certain times. Thinking back... on personal tribal stories and the history of my culture figures into how I organize my music." he says.

Sandra Hale Schulman

While solo flute albums such as "Canyon Trilogy" are the core of his work, Nakai is continually joining forces with other musicians. He views collaborations as "philosophical communication between... musicians" and opportunities to explore beyond traditional musical and cultural boundaries.

For example his 1994 "Island of Bows" was recorded with a Japanese group using acoustic and traditional Japanese instruments. This collaboration came about because his Japanese cohorts were looking for "new areas of musical performance... not strictly traditionally oriented."

An on-going fraternity of Nakai's is Jackalope, a culturally diverse jazz ensemble with several recordings to their name, which was founded by Larry Yañez and Nakai. The group's music, self-described as "synthacousticpunkarachiNavajazz" and uses electronic and modern instruments mixed with traditional, ethnic instruments allowing Nakai to "break the rules".

Nakai has been nominated for Grammys and won a Nammy in 1998. He has written and performed scores for film and television including selections for the National Park Service, Fox Television, the

Discovery Channel, IMAX, the National Geographic Society and many commercial productions.

Since 1990, Nakai has also collaborated with pianist Peter Kater. Together they have recorded four albums, *Natives, How the West Was Lost, Honorable Sky* and *Migrations* (winner of the 1992 Indie Award).

In 1992, Nakai received the Governor of Arizona's Arts Award, the second Native American so honored. In 1994, Nakai was conferred with an honorary doctorate by Northern Arizona University and the Arizona Board of Regents for his exceptional achievements and contributions to humankind.

In 1995, "Feather, Stone & Light," a musical trialogue with longtime collaborators William Eaton and Will Clipman, was noted as a Billboard Critic's Choice and quickly debuted on Billboard's Top New Age Albums chart, remaining there for 13 weeks. Nakai once again broke new ground in the fall of 1996 when he debuted his first jazz album, "A Kokopelli's Cafe," featuring The R. Carlos Nakai Quartet.

Sandra Hale Schulman

A prolific musician and composer, he has more than 27 albums in commercial distribution, including 18 releases on the Canyon Records label. Just counting his Canyon titles, Nakai recently surpassed the 2,000,000 units sold worldwide.

When he is not recording, composing or researching, 70 to 80 percent of the year is spent touring throughout the U.S., Canada, Europe and Japan performing and lecturing on Native American culture and philosophy. Nakai says:

"We were put on the earth to experience life in its totality. And if you're not doing that, you're essentially wasting your time."

A big man, both physically and in his field, **Robert Tree Cody** is a flutist, dancer, artist, educator and actor. He has performed throughout the United States, Europe, Canada, Scandinavia, the United Kingdom, the Far East., Central and South America. A prize winning traditional dancer, the 6 foot 10 inch Cody is well known on the pow wow circuit as a northern traditional dancer, master of ceremonies and arena director.

From Kokopellis to Electric Warriors
The Native American Culture of Music

In 1978, he was presented with the Queen's 25th Silver Jubilee Medal for his command performance as a Fancy and Eagle Dancer for the Queen of England. Cody has lectured at museums, schools, universities and colleges. As a counselor and educator, Cody frequently participates in artist-in-residence programs at elementary and middle schools for the Arizona Commission on the Arts. Of Maricopa-Dakota heritage, Cody has taught students of all ages about the folklore, crafts, music and traditional ways of Native American people.

Tree has a remarkable ability in communicating with people, particularly young people of all cultures. He has given generously of his time and talents for benefits of people in need.

A versatile flute player, Cody has five albums on the Canyon Records label. Current albums include White Buffalo, which features thirteen songs for the Native American flute, with keyboardist Rob Wallace and percussionist Will Clipman, combining their different musical perspectives into a new expression inspired by the traditions that honors the spirit of the buffalo; and Maze, which tells of a musical journey in the Southwest.

Sandra Hale Schulman

At the 1999 Nammy show in Albuquerque, Cody performed a powerful flute duet with Xavier and was moved to tears when he won an award, movingly thanking his wife and family.

Benito Concha is a dynamic world class drummer out of Taos, New Mexico who makes his own drums and is a well regarded traditional dancer. Moving easily through a variety of musical styles, Concha has shared the stage with Santana, Blues Traveler, Jackson Browne, Ziggy Marley, and many more.

He performed on the 1996 HORDE tour, critics called his performances with the 1997 Red Sky Production's presentation of TRIBE, 'electrifying' and 'show-stopping'. He was artistic director for an emotionally charged, sold-out performance with the Kodo drummers at the '98 Earth Celebration in Japan. He also directed a Secret Souls / Red Willow dancers show in Tokyo to another capacity audience.

Benito has been in several bands, including Red Thunder and Secret Souls, and has served as an organizer for the Native Roots & Rhythms Festival in New Mexico.

From Kokopellis to Electric Warriors
The Native American Culture of Music

Kevin Locke, Lakota fluist

Kevin Locke is known throughout the world as the pre-eminent player of the indigenous traditional Northern Plains flute, as well as an inspiring Hoop Dancer, storyteller, educator, and recording artist.

His Lakota name is Tokeya Inajin, which means "The First To Arise." Reared on the Standing Rock Sioux Reservation (Hunkpapa Band of Lakota) in South Dakota, he lived with his elderly uncle Abraham End of Horn whose first language was Lakota and who gave the boy early training in the traditions of his culture.

As a teenager, Kevin turned to his elders for guidance and wisdom. He was generously rewarded with gifts of music, stories and, above all, spirit. Ever since that experience, Kevin has felt compelled to share those gifts with the world.

Locke also holds a Master of Arts degree in Educational Administration from the University of South Dakota, where he was ready to begin law school before realizing that music and dance are his destiny. Said by many to be a living "channel" to the ancient music, Kevin is an exquisite player of the indigenous cedarwood flute. He is a musical hero and role model to American Indian youth across all of North America, and younger players are frequently waiting backstage, eager to be with him, to ask and to learn.

Along with Nakai, he has been a pivotal force in the powerful revival of the indigenous flute tradition, which teetered on the brink of extinction a mere thirty years ago.

Kevin Locke came to national attention first as a hoop dancer, a performer in another ancient and honorable Lakota tradition. In this physically complex and acrobatic dance, the dancer whirls within twirling hoops, explicating the native view of the world as hoops intersect and grow into ever more revealing designs that show the way of life.

Kevin's special joy is working with children, especially on the reservations and reserves, to ensure the survival, growth and well-being of native culture. He is often joined onstage in song and dance by his daughters Kimimila and Waniya, along with his son Ohiyesa.

In 1990 Kevin was awarded a National Heritage Fellowship by the National Endowment for the Arts which recognized him as a "Master Traditional Artist who has contributed to the shaping of our artistic traditions and to preserving the cultural diversity of the United States." Kevin has performed in nearly 70 countries, sharing his vision of music and dance as balance, joy and diversity. Deeply committed to the conservation of Earth's resources for future generations, he was a delegate to the 1992 Earth Summit in Brazil and a featured performer and speaker at the 1996 United Nations Habitat II Conference in Turkey.

"It is incredible to see the beauty of the people on this Earth and the vast richness of humankind," he says from his home in the Wakpala district of the Standing Rock Reservation. "All of the people have the same impulses, spirits, and goals."

Kevin's home in the Wakpala district of the Standing Rock Reservation overlooks the Missouri River near Mobridge, South Dakota.

Brent Michael Davids

"…a fresh, lilting score"

Lynn Voedisch - Chicago Sun Times

"…unmatched texture and resonance"

    Betty Webb - Phoenix Tribune

"…a whippoorwill score…"

    Sid Smith - Chicago Tribune

"…thought-provoking mystery, steeped in tradition"

    Daniel Buckley - Tucson Citizen

As his glowing reviews attest, Brent Michael Davids is one of the finest young composers in America. His award-winning compositions bear an unmistakable Native American impression. The Singing Woods, written for the Kronos Quartet, and Moon of the Falling Leaves, for the Joffrey Ballet, are both inspired by traditional Mohican life.

Davids is no stranger to Western European composition; he is one of the few classically-trained Native American composers working today. His appetite for experimentation and deep connection with indigenous music, in combination with his 18 years as a composer, explain why he receives commissions from the nation's best-known ensembles.

In many of his works, Davids promotes cross-cultural understanding and appreciation for indigenous lifeways. His Voices of Shadow Canyon, for example, conveys his encounter with the people and petroglyphs of Canyon De Chelly in northern Arizona. In all his works, Davids translates the sounds of his imagination into a musical experience for others by creating distinctively original instruments such as soprano and bass flutes made of quartz crystal.

Premiering in New York in the late 1990s, Davids' second commission for the Kronos Quartet, Turtle People, featured the Mohican creation story and a turtle water drum.

In addition to his 1992 compact disc release, Ni-Tcang, he has published a composition for a youth choir, Mohican Friends, that teaches introductory vocal sounds, words and phrases in the Mohican language.

Branscombe Richmond and Robert Tree Cody, photo by Kimberlie R. Hall

From Kokopellis to Electric Warriors
The Native American Culture of Music

Chapter Four

Themes and Visions

There are major themes that make up the collective spirit of modern music makers: a desire for homelands, spiritual reverence, family, animals as spirits, ethnic pride, treaty violations, politics.

These are images of inspiration: photos of modern reservations, bingo parlors, native children, Powwows, drumming circles, art by Stephen Tiger and Damian Rojo, photos of the Santa Fe flea market cactus and landscapes, and one of the most beautiful final resting places in the world - Taos Pueblo graveyard.

Sandra Hale Schulman

**Indian Head with Stars
Mixed Media artwork by Damian Rojo**

From Kokopellis to Electric Warriors
The Native American Culture of Music

Multi-culture mix up in Cherokee, NC

Pow Wow South Dakota

Sandra Hale Schulman

Wild Cactus – Abiquio, NM May 1995, photo by S. Schulman

From Kokopellis to Electric Warriors
The Native American Culture of Music

Pow-wow dancers, South Dakota

Taos Pueblo graveyard, May 1995, photo by Schulman

Skulls and bandanas, Santa Fe flea market, May 1995, photo by Schulman

From Kokopellis to Electric Warriors
The Native American Culture of Music

Pow-wow, South Dakota

Miccosukee girl, 12/96, photo by S. Schulman

Sandra Hale Schulman

Skulls, drums and crosses at the Santa Fe Flea Market

Bishops Lodge, Santa Fe, NM

From Kokopellis to Electric Warriors
The Native American Culture of Music

Teaching the Young, pencils & acrylic paint, Stephen Tiger, 1978

Sandra Hale Schulman

Secrets, pencils & acrylic paint, Stephen Tiger, 1978

From Kokopellis to Electric Warriors
The Native American Culture of Music

Ghost Horse
Bill Milier

Sandra Hale Schulman

Chapter Five

Native Rock On A Roll

In the 1950s in America, rock music evolved from black culture based blues, crossed over and became the sound of white youth's rebellion and social enlightenment. Elvis Presley, raised in Tennessee and one of the pioneers of rock, was part Native American. Taking their cue from the rebellious sounds of rock and the surge of Indian activism, starting in the 1970's a new generation of Native Americans began turning to Native rock to carry their message to the younger generations.

Some, like California's Redbone, have been enormously successful and others, most notably Flagstaff's BLACKFIRE, have been extremely controversial. Many others simply assimilated into the mainstream music population without drawing attention to their heritage. Ironically Robbie Robertson, a member of The Band in the 1980s, became known for writing songs on the European American

From Kokopellis to Electric Warriors
The Native American Culture of Music

experience like the Civil Wars and western expansion, but in the past five years has returned to song writing as a link between his Mohawk heritage and his musical career.

With much of popular forms of music like country and folk going back to their beginnings, it was inevitable that Native Americans would combine the roots of their heritage with the wings of rock music. The result is powerful music that attempts to restore a sense of balance to the musicians lives and causes.

Major music labels and TV music shows have received overwhelming responses whenever they air these groups. In this age of cable TV, satellite transmissions and compact discs, the music makers must use these tools for the message to thrive.

Like all the other forms of Indian music and their stories, native rock is rooted in the reservations.

Deep in the heart of the Everglades on a sweltering summer day in 1995, the past and the present in native rock met on a concert stage when Miami's Miccosukee Indian group **Tiger Tiger** played with Redbone, the most successful Native American rock band in history.

Sandra Hale Schulman

The occasion was the 20th Annual Everglades Music Festival, an event the Miccosukees hold to help communication between Indian and non-Indian people and also to raise funds for their educational programs.

Redbone is the only Native American band to be inducted into the Rock and Roll Hall of Fame, whose multi-million dollar home is on the banks of Lake Erie in Cleveland, Ohio. They have been around for over 20 years, their blues laden pop rock sound produced the huge hit "Come and Get Your Love" in the 1970s, they have gone on to sell millions of albums and tour the country. In February 1994 they were awarded the First Native American Arts Award.

But the heights to which Redbone have risen is a far cry from their beginnings as the children of crop pickers, moving from migrant camp to migrant camp with their families in Southern California.

Realizing this was a dead end street, Yuqui Indian brothers Patrick and Lolly Vegas began writing songs together as teenagers, and playing in a band they called Redbone from a Cajun word meaning half breed Native American.

They began getting gigs backing blues performers Odetta and John Lee Hooker, songs they wrote were more in the soul pop vein and were recorded by Aretha Franklin, Bobbie Gentry, The Righteous Brothers.

Desiring to make more of a name for themselves, they holed up for a year writing and recording, then released an album that hit big with songs "Come and Get Your Love" and "Witch Queen of New Orleans". The groups Louisiana location made their music blues based rock, which gradually gave way to a more homogenized pop sound.

Redbone has sold over 22 million albums and toured constantly for close to two decades, appearing at many festivals, and on TV in Don Kirschner's Rock Concert in the 1970s.

Live the band is an amazing act, dressing in full Indian regalia and playing a tightly sewn crazy quilt of jazz, blues, pop and rock. They even throw in some Indian language chanting towards the end of the set.

But Redbone has played the game the American way, preferring to subliminate their personal tribal politics to make headway in the mainstream American music industry.

Cutting back on their schedule, Redbone now primarily plays the reservation casino circuit despite the controversies that split the tribes on the issue of whether casinos are their biggest mistake or their greatest salvation. Many previous fans of the group are surprised to learn they still exist, as the casino and reservation circuit is another world unto itself. In 1995 they released an album call Redbone Live on the WEA label.

Sharing the stage with Redbone that summer were Stephen and Lee Tiger of Tiger Tiger, a band of Miccosukee Indian brothers who live in the Everglades on the Miccosukee Reservation. They have been making music for personal and social reasons since the 1960's, playing festivals with Cream, Chicago, the Grateful Dead, Led Zeppelin and Eric Clapton.

Tiger Tiger appeared in the movie "Band of the Hand" in the mid 80's (with drummer Paul Deakin of multiplatinum country roots group The Mavericks), and wrote the music for a National Geographic special.

"Back in the 60's it made us think that the elusive fame and fortune thing was right around the corner." says Stephen Tiger. "But 12 years of touring an elusive road burned us out."

"That's when we had a shift in consciousness and decided to come home to Florida and get back to our tribe. We started creating benefits and concerts to raise awareness and create a positive image of our people."

The band is now self managed and they only play about 3 or 4 times a year, concentrating instead on recording and working with the tribe. The SOAR Corporation out of Albuquerque helped release Tiger Tiger's 1993 album "Tamiami Station", renamed "Space Age Indian", on CD to wider distribution in 1998.

The lyrics to the title song written by Stephen Tiger tell their story:

> I've been changing and I know you see
> But still you stereotype me on your big TV

Sandra Hale Schulman

I don't kill soldiers and I don't fight bears

The only damn scalp I got is in my hair

I've been educated

Took time but I made it

I like my computer

I'm a space age Indian

I won't be left behind

I'm changing with the time

My feet's in the culture, I fly in a jet

the sky's the limit and I'm doing my best

I drive a car used to use a canoe

I'm a spiritual being but I ain't too cool for school

I used to live by hunting

No shoes when I was running

But now the Everglades is changing

Someone rearranged them

Space age Indian

I won't be left behind

I'm changing with the time

From Kokopellis to Electric Warriors
The Native American Culture of Music

Learning about the non-Indian ways

I had to be taught the old Indian days

Head for the future while we cling to the past

Mix them together and our nation will last

Can't live like we used to

As much as we would love to

We still love Mother Nature

I would never waste her

I'm a space age Indian

You saw me on TV

Soldiers shoot 'em down

But I'm still here you see

No more tomahawk

No more tears for me

I won't cry 'em now

Cause I know what you see

—Space Age Indian by Tiger Tiger

Sandra Hale Schulman

Twenty five miles out into the Everglades on Route 41, Stephen Tiger runs the public relations offices of the Miccosukee Tribe from his roadside Tamiami Trail office. The walls are lined with photos of a thirty year career. There are bright surreal paintings Stephen Tiger has done of native scenes - one of which is the cover of the "Space Age Indian". It depicts a proudly decorated American bald eagle as the space shuttle from Cape Canaveral shoots into the stratosphere over his white feathered head.

There are beaded patchwork costumes, guitars, press clippings and photos of performances around the world. There is also a computer, VCR and CD player. Lee Tiger works out of South Miami on promotions for swamp safari's and Seminole Indian events.

The Tiger brothers have been at this game a long time, realizing the need to combine teaching and culture preservation with art and music.

"We're isolated down here," Stephen Tiger concurs," but we found out about SOAR and are happy to be in wider distribution. It seems that Indian music is in the same state as reggae was years ago, so new nobody knew what to do with it. In Miami we get overshadowed by black and Latin music, we are an older but much smaller minority. I have trouble getting groups down for our annual festivals because it is so geographically inconvenient, we are basically in the water out here."

Growing up the Tiger brothers were taught Miccosukee language first, then English. Their father, who became the first chief of the tribe after their official government recognition in 1963, never saw a white man until the Tamiami Trail went in around 1939, cutting across the state through areas that had been inaccessible except by canoe for hundreds of years.

"We listened to spiritual music in the 60's, so we sing of our heritage", says Stephen," but we play rock songs. Music is a great vehicle for getting across a message of understanding and getting around stereotypes people have of Native Americans."

The Miccosukee were not even recognized by the government until 1962; so complete was their isolation out in the inhospitable Florida swamps. The tribe is originally part of the Creek Nation, with a history in Florida that dates back to the 1600s. Their verbal history was passed down in the language of "Mikasuki".

Being as engulfed by nature as they are, the tribe is represented by their flag of yellow, red, black and white that represents the circle of life- east, west, north and south. Many of the tribe still live in chickee huts, but many more live in small concrete block houses and work in either the small self contained village or in the sprawling casino on Krome Ave.

Their way of life was simple for hundreds of years until the city of Miami was founded in the late 1890s and people slowly started canvasing the rest of the state.

"Tamiami Trail came through in 1939," Stephen says "then fishing boats, then beer cans came floating by, airplanes overhead. Nothing was sacred anymore. We had to fight for our land even though it had no plumbing or electricity. Our story is different than the plains and northern Indians, we never had bloody wars, we just retreated into the glades where no one wanted the land, but to us it was paradise."

"I remember reaching out my back door and being able to catch fish or game. We were here watching the change over the years and put it to music. I like to think we've brought some positive attention to what is happening out here, we bring school children for tours and lectures, I teach and organize festivals. I'm trying to equate the old and new ways of lives."

Tiger Tiger's next album to be released by SOAR is "Dream Scout", the first song is "The Painters Song" where he likens songwriting to the painting process, taking the reality and the spirituality he sees and making it into art.

Tiger Tiger's time is coming around again, ideas of Indians in the space age have been in Stephen's head for 20 years.

"I think people are searching for a more basic lifestyle," says Lee Tiger, "they want lives that are more ecology minded, more spiritual with alternative religions. We have a medicine man here, our religions are based on the elements, learning to co-exist and respect nature."

"Our church is the land," says Stephen, "the concept of owning land was foreign to us, but we had to play the game to survive. All this finds its way into the music's message, I get a lot of students and university people who want to know these things from the source. Our greatest joy is playing the music, but so many other things are a priority too. we're normal people who value our heritage while trying to raise families, make a living and move along with the times. It's that ability to adapt that allows us to survive."

While Tiger Tiger struggles to keep playing together and teach their small tribe, events like their annual craft and music festivals bring their message to the outside world. Now their nationally distributed CD will take them out on the road again, full circle. The circle of life.

BLACKFIRE is a Native American (DinÈ) traditionally influenced, high-energy, politically driven group comprised of three stunning siblings bass player Jeneda, Clayson the drummer, and guitarist and lead singer Klee.

Born into the heart of a political land dispute area called Big Mountain on the Navajo Nation, this family's powerful music reflects the hopes, freedoms, and barriers of today's world. The band's style is comprised of traditional Native American, punk, ska and alternative music with strong sociopolitical messages about government oppression, relocation of indigenous people, eco-cide, genocide, domestic violence and human rights. The band has toured the US,

Canada and Europe and at every stop they strongly promote the respect of all cultures. They do many workshops, lectures and school residencies, and they play only at all ages venues, whether concerts, festivals or clubs.

One of their main supporters was the Godfather of Punk music Joey Ramone. He became so enamored of the band he had them play at one of his infamous Blitzkreig concerts in New York City and sang on their CD "One Nation Under."

In July 2000, less than a year before he died, Joey, who I had known from my underground NY days in the 1970s, sent me an email.

In it he wrote:

"Hello Sandra, hope you're well and all is good. I'm doing some work with this really cool unique band called BLACKFIRE. They're Navajo Indian – 2 brothers and a sister, their father Jones Benally is a very famous Medicine Man and a key figure of the Navajo tribe in Arizona. BLACKFIRE blend traditional music and culture with Punk rock and are very politically active – the father chants on a few tunes which gives me the chills – they are in the process of recording their first full album being produced by Don Flemming of Sonic Youth. I am going to do some vocals as well with these very talented, beautiful kids that are refreshingly down to earth. You have to check them out – they currently have a 5 song CD out on a French label but I say wait to hear what they're doing now – when the kids aren't playing music they do traditional dance with their father Jones Benally. Now Arturo (the Ramones art director) tells me you're working for a Native American organization – you really have to check them out – can I put you in touch with them?

All the best Joey Ramone."

BLACKFIRE's independent releases in the U.S. on Tacoho Records is also available in Europe on Wowoka (Musicdisc).

This photogenic group was recently featured in a twelve page cover story in France's *Best* magazine, and they also have a twenty page article in *L'uomo Vogue*, among many other articles in numerous other publications. BLACKFIRE's exciting and original music is sometimes combined with their Native American dance troupe, the

Jones Benally Family, to create a performance entitled "Living in Both Worlds."

BLACKFIRE'S MANIFESTO

We are at critical times. Our traditional teachings and our ways of life are hanging by a thread.

For centuries, war has been waged against our people. The United States government has committed crime upon crime against humanity.

Our lives are evidence, our teachings hold the testimony, we are not a page forgotten in a history book. But we are written between the lines, swept under this Imperialistic carpet.

Today, we still are within reach of our traditional teachings. There are elders who still hold strong to these teachings. We are losing these people and when they are gone who will we learn our traditions from? This is something you cannot learn in books. Schools can teach you what you are but, not who. This comes from your parents, your ancestry.

Our ancestors, our grandparents did not die for us to watch T.V. and drink our lives away. Our ancestors had a choice. They could have given in and bowed their heads in submission but, they did not. Our ancestors had a choice. They thought of the coming generations. Our ancestors thought of us. We have a responsibility to honor the struggles they endured; to use these tools given to us. Why must we be forced to choose between tradition and this modern world.

We must embrace them both because, there is only one world, crossed by many different paths. We can still retain our cultural heritage and walk in this modern world. We are all Indigenous to somewhere; Asia, Africa, Europe, The Americas, all continents. We all have the blood of a traditional culture flowing through our veins, no matter how mixed or how pure, You just have to acknowledge it. "For our children." these words have been last words, battle cries, compromises, and now these words are ours. How shall we honor them?

©1994 Tacoho productions ASCAP

"That's what I feel I do, I write American mythology. I'm the storyteller of the shadowland."—**Robbie Robertson**

From Kokopellis to Electric Warriors
The Native American Culture of Music

Robertson had been a follower of modern American Indian music for years, since his mother took him to her native Mohawk reservations in Ontario when he was a child. There is where he first saw musicians up close.

"They were astounding in their connection to Mother Earth, they were so spiritual. They could forecast the weather and literally run up trees. My relatives played guitars, mandolins, my cousin showed me my first chords there." Robertson says. "It turned my life around. I didn't get into music because of Elvis, I got into it because of Cousin Herb. I thought, O I gotta have some of that."

He formed a group called The Hawks, then when they hooked up with Bob Dylan they simply became The Band in 1965. The music was a mixture of white gospel, bluegrass, carnival, folk and soft rock music. Robertson's lyrics to songs Up On Cripple Creek, The Night They Drove Old Dixie Down, The Shape I'm In- so touched the imagination of the American heartland, no one knew he was Canadian or Native American.

But for The Band success, drugs and touring wore the best of them down, a final concert was filmed by Martin Scorcese, it was called The Last Waltz and also starred Dylan, Joni Mitchell, Neil Young and Muddy Waters.

After that Robertson, and his stories, were out on their own.

When the opportunity to pen the soundtrack for a Turner Broadcasting Service (TBS) documentary series on "The Native Americans" came along in 1994 "I was just the right man for the job," he told Rolling Stone.

Robertson's compositions over the years since he left his group in the 1980s had been laden with offerings to his half- Mohawk heritage. He had been visiting reservations in New Mexico and said he listened to the artists who had such pride in their heritage, they are, he says "offering a strong new voice."

Songs from that period of solo writing like "Hell's Half Acre" tells the story of an Indian who goes off to fight with white society and returns with a ravaged soul. And "Broken Arrow" asks the directions of a spiritual quest:

> Who else is going to bring you
> A broken arrow?

From Kokopellis to Electric Warriors
The Native American Culture of Music

Who else is going to bring you

A bottle of rain

There he goes

Moving across the water

There he goes

Turning my whole world around

—Broken Arrow® by Robbie Robertson, 1987

A weighty presence on film (The Last Waltz, Carny, Going Home) Robertson still feels the calling as the music messenger.

When TBS called for the soundtrack he was way ahead of the game, gathering talent from across the country - calling on Kashtin from Canada, Ulali from Manhattan, Benito Concha from Taos - and put together a record that would attempt to show the breadth of artistry that exists today among American Indian musicians.

But what would come out of all this gathering, dubbed the Red Road Ensemble, was initially unknown. Flute player Douglas Spotted Eagle, who has many records out on the SOAR label, was one of the biggest revelations to Robertson, as he came in with a handmade flute and a computer and synthesizer keyboards.

"He's a very modern musician," he says "who also plays the flute, a very primitive instrument. He wasn't trying to be anything other than what he is."

The results of the collaborative work are elegiac, a spooky, spiritual flow of drumbeats and chants and words sung in obscure native languages.

The tone was kept particularly low key as Robertson "didn't want to write sympathetic feel sorry for me music like "you took my land, you mistreated me.' We all know that story, but it is much more powerful to praise great poets and spokesman and warriors."

> Crazy Horse was a mystic
> He knew the secret of the trance
> And Sitting Bull the great Apostle
> of the Ghost Dance
> You don't stand a chance against my prayers
> You don't stand a chance against my love

From Kokopellis to Electric Warriors
The Native American Culture of Music

They outlawed The Ghost dance

But we shall live again,

We shall live again

—Ghost Dance® by Robbie Robertson and Jim Wilson

The recording session took Robertson from one end of the country to the other, using crickets, wind, stomping feet and lyrics inspired by stories of tribal warriors Chief Joseph of the Nez Perce. Legends like the Navajo tale of the Skin Walker - a being who has the power to enter souls, became entire songs. Cherokee Morning Song was one that had been passed down in singer Rita Coolidges family for generations. It was sung on the record by Rita, her daughter, her sister and her niece. That group, minus Rita's daughter, would later become the group Walela.

"All the impressions that are made come from somewhere long ago." says Robertson. "They're old stuff I'd done over the years, writing stories of the past. It was ideal for me to do something that I have a knack for. The people that I worked with were all in that same place too."

Sandra Hale Schulman

Cherokee Reservation Fall Festival & Pow Wow, October 6, 1996: **Keith Secola and the Wild Band of Indians** of Tempe Arizona

Take a long, leisurely drive up Route 441 through Florida, Georgia and into the Carolinas. Past places named the Pickin Parlor Lounge, Hunger and Hardship Creek, Apple Pie Ridge Road and the Big Sandy Baptist Church.

Through the mountains around a bend and into Cherokee, North Carolina, a town of almost obscene extremes. While it is a genuine reservation and community of the Eastern Band of Cherokee, it has sold part of it's soul to appease the tourist gods, a mighty but lesser diety of modern America.

It's almost painful to see inns named the Redskin Motel, and big clumsy paper mache statues of buffalo along the roadside next to canvas teepees. Buffalo and teepees belong way out west, not in the Smoky Mountain land of log cabins and black bears.

From Kokopellis to Electric Warriors
The Native American Culture of Music

And pity the poor back bear, a normally fearsome creature whose claws and hearts and heads are prized as symbols of strength and virility. Here in Cherokee bears are penned in wire fenced cages, begging for apples and stale white bread while parades of people take their pictures and hold their noses against the stench. It's almost comic in a way, this side-by-side sideshow of gaudy totem poles, painted souvenir teepees and dancing bear zoos.

But beyond the roadside attractions lives and breathes a real community, with schools, a library, museum and historical center. A sparkling river runs through it, filled with sleek shiny trout and fat quacking ducks. The hazy Smoky Mountains rise above it, mute and grand.

Every October Cherokee throws itself a Fall Festival - filling the fairgrounds with music, carnival rides, exhibits and a Pow Wow.

A sense of humor is needed to play this schizophrenic town, in 1996 that bill was filled by Keith Secola and His Wild Band of Indians who came to Cherokee to play the Festival and do special shows for groups of kids at the elementary and high schools.

Sandra Hale Schulman

Secola is the writer of "NDN Cars" (or Indian Cars), a song that has reached near anthem status in the Native American music world. His ode to traditional foods is the song "Fry Bread". A real charmer, it's sweet and funny and a perfect sing-a-long song.

An Anishinable Indian from Minnesota who is also part Italian, Secola has been performing since 1990, evolving into one of the top Native bands in America and Europe. Using an electric guitar and pop wow drums, Secola blends traditional and new sounds into a powerful contemporary "organic" mix.

His music has been heard in the film "Dance Me Outside", in the 1998 "Rockin Warriors" film and on the "Honor The Earth" compilation CD by the Indigo Girls. He has put out his own CDs: "For Our Ancestors," "Indian Cars", and 1999's "Finger Monkey".

Secolas sly sense of humor (see band title) coupled with his renegade looks has served him well as an artist to be reckoned with, but who doesn't take himself too seriously. Sitting in the office of the Festival, Secola spoke about his music and what road he's trying to take it on.

From Kokopellis to Electric Warriors
The Native American Culture of Music

"My music is universal whether it's on or off the rez," Secola says, "the songs are the definition of metaphysical understanding- it means one thing to me and might mean something different to someone else. A song when its written, someone could say he's talking about my car, my friend, my situation. Native people relate to this because a lot of it is topical and political. Mainstream America who are into Neil Young or Bob Marley can relate to the folk aspect- people who are making a difference."

"The drumbeat is the heart of the sound here. Kids love this too, I have two children and keep them in mind when I write, our fan base is from kids to elders, but the electric guitar and beat attracts all, its organic and natural for me here- an organic process.

I grew up in northern Minnesota, near Bob Dylan's home town. All those years I heard folk, acoustic, bluegrass, gospel music- music that's at the core of a lot of Indian influences. I grew up with Native music and am a part of it all, pop radio too, but at powwows I was singing all the time. It's very organic for me to synthesize the music, music is music, it wasn't compartmentalized like this is White music, this is Black music, this is Chicano music. There were no boundaries. It's natural. Taking pow wow music into what we're doing is easy."

"The drum has four or five basic beats from the crow hop to the war dance. The beat is simple but melodies are complex, almost like jazz or African music, I vary into both with complex beats, simple melodies and simple beats but complex melodies."

"I combine Indian singing with my folk melodies, there's a lot of power there, it covers a lot of ground. As a song writer I try not to make it too religious though. What I want to do is take it (Native music) out of new age and into rock age, there's just too much flute playing lately, which has its place but what we're doing is making it more modern. I could cash it on it, get a flute and wear the buckskins and tell a story, but there's more to be done than that."

"I've played with Neil Young in Denmark, the Red Hot Chili Peppers, Patti Smith, David Bowie and that's gotten me mainstream exposure. Crossing the music over, I'd like to think people are more open to roots music of all types but the truth is some people want to keep their stereo types and myths, that's why I named our band Wild Band as a gentle joke, we're more of a Mild Band - addressing respect, roots, new opportunities. I write about what many others write about, universal truth too, love."

"The goal is to record more and release a CD in 1997, (which Secola did) do some touring in Canada. Mickey Hart of the Grateful Dead was ready to produce us, the deal was set four days before Jerry Garcia died but it's been on hold since."

"We had several songs on the soundtrack of the Miramax film "Dance Me Outside" directed by Norman Jewison and produced by Kevin Costner, it ran on Showtime (and is now available through SOAR Records). The movie was made with Indian actors, it's a cult hit now. We're off to Europe for some shows, we'll use native dancers and a 5 piece band with costumes."

"As always I'm excited about our music, and I feel what what we're doing is unique in combining the genres."

In 2000 Secola hooked up John Densmore, drummer for The Doors, and has continued to tour and hang out with kids on the rez.

Sandra Hale Schulman

Tiger Tiger, Alternative Indian Rock

From Kokopellis to Electric Warriors
The Native American Culture of Music

Redbone

Blackfire

Sandra Hale Schulman

Robbie Robertson

From Kokopellis to Electric Warriors
The Native American Culture of Music

Keith Secola and Cherokee Kids

Sandra Hale Schulman

Keith Secola and the Wild Band of Indians

Chapter Six

Indian / Country

Country music, often called the white mans blues, is not always created by whites. Living in the American South, the majority of people there can trace their relatives to at least one, if not more, Native tribes. The most legendary performers of country music, readily admit to their native roots, even though their music gives only a passing toe tapping nod to it.

The usual reason is that those born in the early 1900s entered the world during a time when Southern Indian reservations had long been extinguished or evacuated to the plains of the west. Many Natives moved into more urban areas, intermarrying and dropping traditional lifestyles. Life became integrated into the typical small town existence of farming, coal mining or working rail road lines. There was also a major economic depression during the 1930s, and life everywhere became a harder row to hoe.

Loretta Lynn was born right into all this on April 14, 1935, a coal miner's daughter, the second of the eight children of Ted and Clara Webb. She is one-quarter Cherokee on her moms side, and her name came from Clara's fondness for film star, Loretta Young.

In Lynn's new book "Still Woman Enough" she talks about her Indian grandfather.

"His real name was Nathaniel Ramey," she writes, "the Ramey part being changed from the Indian name of Raney. Grandpa was a full-blood Cherokee Indian. Indians didn't talk much in those days. They just sat real quiet and stared into space like they was thinking a lot. I think the Indians was still bitter about the way the white man cheated them out of most of this country in the 1800s, and I don't blame them one bit. About all my Indian grandpa did was sit in a rocker, smoke a pipe, and grunt. If you spoke to him he'd grunt some more."

Lynn was raised in a small shack in Butcher Hollow, Kentucky during the Depression and was attracted to country music as an 11-year-old, when the family acquired a radio and she heard the singing of Molly O'Day.

Her autobiography tells of her handmade wardrobe, hardscrabble life and how, at the age of 13, she married a serviceman, Oliver Vanetta Lynn, known to his friends as Doolittle or Mooney, which was short for Moonshine. He took her to Custer, Washington, and she had four children and several miscarriages by the time she was 18. They had a total of six children and Lynn was a grandmother at the age of 29. 'Mooney', recognizing her talent, encouraged her to sing in local clubs and her band, the Trailblazers, included her brother, Jay Lee Webb, on guitar.

"After Doo shoved me into it, I knew I had to do it, to prove to him that I could. He said I could, and I didn't want to let him down," Lynn says in her down home, hard twang way.

Lynn began with cover songs, but soon began "writing rhymes" as she calls it, stories from her life and the lives of people around her. Most songs centered on the tough reality of relationships, but she touched on social issues as well, about feminism and birth control and being on the road by herself.

Her talent was recognized by Don Grashey of Zero Records, who took her to Los Angeles in February 1960 where she recorded four of her own songs. Zero had zero money for promotion, so she and Mooney promoted her first single, "I'm A Honky Tonk Girl," themselves, the song taking its style from Kitty Wells's "It Wasn't God Who Made Honky Tonk Angels." Mooney said that they drove 80,000 miles to sell 50,000 copies, but it reached number 14 in the US country charts and enabled her to appear regularly on the Grand Ole Opry in Nashville.

Many female singers were jealous of her success, but Patsy Cline sprang to her defense and they became close friends. (Lynn released a tribute album to her in 1977.)

When they moved to Nashville, she became a regular on a weekly television show with the Wilburn Brothers, who also managed her. Kitty Wells and Patsy Cline were two of her major influences and she was thrilled when she was assigned to their producer, Owen Bradley, by USA Decca Records. She had further hits with "Before I'm Over You" and "Blue Kentucky Girl."

Lynn continued on as a feisty writer of her own material, she developed a hard-hitting persona as the wife who stood no nonsense from her rivals (You Ain't Woman Enough, Fist City) or her husband (her first country number 1 "Don't Come Home A-Drinkin (With Lovin On Your Mind") or from her one controversial Indian song, 1966's "Your Squaw Is On The Warpath."

Her best-known record, the autobiographical Coal Miner's Daughter, was a U.S. country number one in 1970. Shel Silverstein, ironically a Playboy cartoonist, wrote "One's On The Way" in which she was harassed by her children and an insensitive husband. She answered Tammy Wynette's "Stand By Your Man" in 1975 with the double standards of "The Pill", which was banned by several USA radio stations. By way of contrast, she subsequently had a country hit with a song called "Pregnant Again."

Although her first duets were with Ernest Tubb, she formed a regular team with Conway Twitty and the combination of the two distinctive voices worked well, especially in "After The Fire Is Gone," "As Soon As I Hang Up The Phone", "The Letter" and the amusingly-titled "You're The Reason Our Kids Are Ugly."

When she fell out with the Wilburn Brothers, she formed United Talent Inc. with Twitty. As the brothers still owned her publishing, she was reluctant to record her own material, although subsequently she was elected to the Nashville Songwriters International Hall of Fame.

In 1972, Lynn was the first woman to become the Country Music Association's Entertainer of the Year and she also shared the Vocal Duo of the Year award with Twitty. In 1973, she made the cover of Newsweek and was the first woman in country music to become a millionaire. Her best-selling autobiography, Coal Miner's Daughter, showed how the human spirit could combat poverty and sickness, but also illustrated that the problems of endless touring could be as traumatic.

Sissy Spacek won an Oscar for her portrayal of Lynn, which included reproducing her singing, in the 1980 film Coal Miner's Daughter, and the film featured Tommy Lee Jones as her husband and Levon Helm of the Band as her father. Her Cherokee mother is portrayed as a dowdy dark haired woman, although Lynn claims the portrayal isn't accurate. Her country music success includes 16 number 1 singles, 60 other hits, 15 number 1 albums and numerous awards. She owns a huge ranch, 70 miles outside of Nashville, which has the whole town of Hurricane Mills in its grounds.

Another part of the property, the Loretta Lynn Dude Ranch, is a tourist attraction with camping facilities. Despite her prolific output in the '60s and '70s, Lynn kept a low profile in the 80s and 90s as she cared for her ailing husband and suffered the loss of her brother and best friend Tammy Wynette.

After grieving for much of the late 1990s, Lynn released a new album in fall of 2000, "Still Country" filled with the kind of country music she has always made - honest, twangy and full of heart.

Hank Williams Sr. was a hard drinking, hard living country singer who packed more classic songs into his 29 years than anyone since. He always said he was part Indian, with the tribes of Cree and Cherokee being most likely. He was born September 17, 1923 in Georgianna, Alabama.

Unlike many other country singers, Williams wrote most of the songs he sang. With time, his songs including "Cold, Cold Heart," and "Your Cheating Heart" have become classics of American music history.

In his lifetime though, Hank Williams Sr. had numerous difficulties. Because of his father's bad health, Williams' family was very poor. His father, Lonnie was a farmer and log trim engineer, his mother, Lilly, was a church organist.

When Williams was seven, his father disappeared, forcing him to work selling peanuts, newspapers and shining shoes to help support his family. By the time he was fourteen, Williams started a country band. His style was influenced by the sounds of gospel, Ernest Tubb, Roy Acuff and the sounds of black music he had learned from a street singer, Rufus "Teetot" Payne, who lived in Williams's home town.

Writing and singing his own songs, Williams won an amateur contest in Montgomery, Alabama for his performance of "WPA Blues," which he wrote. In 1937, Williams formed his own band, the Drifting Cowboys, which played in Alabama honky tonks. Williams's first years in the band where harsh. During World War II he had to quit and work as a welder in shipyards. However, after the war he went back to his true interest, music.

In 1946, Williams and his wife, Audrey, moved to Nashville where they called Fred Rose, Nashville's biggest music writer and publisher. After hearing a few of Willams's songs, Rose immediately signed him to a contract. Under Rose's direction, Williams got a contract with MGM Records and got his first hit "Move It on Over," which landed him a job on a radio show in Shreveport, the "Louisiana Hayride." Rose also helped Williams polish his songs to attract the pop music market.

The Williams-Rose team worked well. "Cold, Cold Heart," one of Williams's tunes, became a no. 1 country hit as well as a pop hit for Tony Benett. Roger Williams said: "It was a perfect union: Williams's native genius, Rose's craftsmanship and sure sense of the market."

Williams songs were a success on the Louisiana Hayride. "I Heard You Crying in Your Sleep," and "Lovesick Blues" were just two of the songs which earned Williams an opportunity to perform on the Grand Ole Opry. His debut, on June 11, 1949, is still considered a major moment in country music history, as he got one encore request after another. Popular demand brought Williams back to the Opry and made him a regular. Williams needed a band to perform with, so he reorganized the Drifting Cowboys and added other studio musicians who traveled with him to do live performances across the U.S., Canada and even to Germany where they entertained American troops.

A year later, the demand for Williams was the highest of any other country star. Songs such as "Why Don't You Love Me?" and "Long Gone Lonesome Blues" became no. 1 hits increasing Williams's popularity even outside the country music sphere. Like Lynn, he wrote songs alluding to Native Americans, like "Kaw Liga", about a drugstore Indian's unrequited love, but it was not really a part of his world.

In 1952, Williams briefly returned to the Louisiana Hayride, divorced his first wife and re-married in a public ceremony that veered on spectacle. On New Year's Eve, 1953, Williams died of a heart attack in the back of a baby blue Cadillac, brought on by years of substance abuse, on his way to Canton, Ohio where he was to perform.

Both of Williams' children, Hank Jr. and Jett, have followed in the foot steps of their legendary father. Hank Jr.s, son Shelton Hank Williams III, is a son of a gun take three, and has launched a

From Kokopellis to Electric Warriors
The Native American Culture of Music

blistering music career of his own. More on Hank III in the Native American Music Awards show chapter.

There are many more country/folk/rock performers like Elvis Presley, Tanya Tucker, Billy Ray Cyrus, the Neville Brothers, Stevie Ray Vaughn and Ray Price who all have native blood.

As music children of the South, their roots run deep into Indian Country.

Sandra Hale Schulman

Hank Williams, Sr.

From Kokopellis to Electric Warriors
The Native American Culture of Music

Photos courtesy of Mercury Records Hank Williams Box Set

Sandra Hale Schulman

Loretta Lynn on her farm in the 1970s, photos copyright Raeanne Rubenstein

Sandra Hale Schulman

Chapter Seven

Nashville's Trail of Hope October 10, 1998

This is where I live.

Along the 1838 Trail of Tears that ran from Georgia and the Carolinas to western Oklahoma sits Nashville, Tennessee, a green little city that straddles a twisted stretch of the Cumberland River. A city named for the Fort and the Army General that drove the Indian population out so European settlers could move into its lush valleys.

The Indian presence has never been very strong in Nashville, a town that first boomed in the late 1800's due to commerce along the muddy banks of the Cumberland River.

A man named Ryman built a church just up the street from the River for the faithful to gather, a church so grand it became the Mother Church and home to country music. Country music being 'white man's blues", string based music that has roots in European fiddles from Scotland, Ireland and England; and came down out of the Appalachian mountains played on home made instruments.

An article in the Tennessean newspaper from 1999 says "One theory about Nashville's musical heritage connects the current boom to Native Americans who thrived on the land years ago. John D. Loudermilk, who's written such hits as 'Then You Can Tell Me Goodbye' and 'Indian Reservation,' suggests there is a strong emotion attached to Indian burial grounds found in the area."

"We know that there were thousands of Indians around in the Nashville area, and for perhaps thousands of years there's been human habitation here. Whenever you dig in Nashville you come across Indian graves. So it's all those dead Indians in the ground. It has to be. Nashville is built on a graveyard, and it's a sadness there that I feel, and I think that writers are picking up on that.

The Native Americans were a very musical people. They had walking songs, running songs, working songs - they lived their lives with a rhythm"

Loudermilk is convinced that in some manner their way of life has seeped into the atmosphere in Nashville.

"Whatever this energy is, there is something under the ground in Nashville, Tennessee that causes this tremendous outpouring of internationally acceptable music." He concludes.

As an extended hand gesture of healing, the National Indian Education Association held their 29th annual conference in Nashville in October 1-14, 1998 with approximately 3,000 Native Americans from nearly 500 tribes in attendance.

While the conference focused on education issues for Indian children, it featured two high profile events - an opening night concert with Bill Miller, John Trudell, Michael Horse, Hal Ketchum, Jimmy Dale Gilmore, Hoop Dancer Lowery Begay, Miss Indian Nations VII, Ulali and actress Irene Bedard. Bedard was a guest at the second event, a screening of the film "Smoke Signals" later in the week.

The scene backstage at the Nashville Arena was a riotous combination of actors, singers, bell jingling dancers and musicians hauling around drums, flutes and guitars. Outfits ranged from cowboy boots, jeans and black leather jackets to shirts festooned with embroidery, bones, bells and ribbons.

From Kokopellis to Electric Warriors
The Native American Culture of Music

It was a gathering that would have been unimaginable twenty, thirty, forty years ago. Political activists, country singers, actors from a mainstream film entirely produced by Native Americans - all sitting, talking, eating and laughing together in a city that had imprisoned and forcibly removed entire tribes a century and a half before.

Yet the conversations centered on music and new CDs, projects, plans, tours and possible collaborations. So many times musicians work alone in a studio or on the road, for them this gathering was a rainbow of wealth in ideas. Ulali's Sonny connected with one of the shows organizers about mating their purebred dogs; top Nashville songwriter Beth Neilsen Chapman asked Bill Miller to co-write with her; Trudell spoke movies and politics with Michael Horse; Irene Bedard talked about current movie soundtracks and her work with Sherman Alexie.

There was even a comedy duo - Williams and Ree, who told off color jokes and played guitar.

While the basis of the show was hope, many of the performers had walked a hard road to get here. Mohican Bill Miller lives in Nashville, having moved there in 1985 from the Stockbridge-Munsee reservation in Wisconsin. He knows the burn of racism in America's melting pot first hand.

"I've encountered people who ask where Pocahontas is, dance around my table going "Woo-Woo" and asking what tribe I'm from. These things in the 90s yet," he says with a heavy sigh.

But Miller's dark skies have also been shot through with light, as he has been sought after as an opening act by groups such as Pearl Jam and Tori Amos. He has had albums released on major US labels. In his performance he played flute, guitar and spoke movingly of his love for his heritage.

"I'm involved with Indian education because it's the only way we can fight back and survive," he says. "My music is native based and always will be, but it's meant for all. I'll always look at the world through an Indian boy's eyes."

Those Indian boys eyes have seen healings by medicine people, vision quests and craftsmen who still hand make canoes.

"It's a part of Native America that is slowly going away." he says.

But it isn't going away with out a fight. Probably the most high profile Indian activist in America today is John Trudell. Santee Sioux poet, musician and one of the most powerful voices in any media, Trudell strides into the Arena like a sharp-suited, sharp tongued beatnik in a dark fitted suit, shades and a beret. Dressed for a war of words, Trudell is in a good mood today, knowing he will have a captive audience of several thousand and many friends, old and new, to greet backstage. He doesn't disappoint, as his rap-speak voice echoes off the back walls, propelled by a heartbeat of a drum and a thousand years of indignity.

Trudell came to prominence as a long time activist for Native American rights and freedoms, as the national spokesperson during the Indians of All Tribes Occupation of Alcatraz Island in 1969, culminating in the formation of AIM (American Indian Movement) in the 70's. He was the National Chairman of AIM, 1973-1979, at a time of enormous turbulence and intensity for Native Americans.

This front page news decade culminated in the siege of Pine Ridge, the Occupation of Wounded Knee, the Jumping Bull Incident (two FBI agents and one Native American were killed) Years of trials and continuous attacks on Trudell and Native Americans followed these events. It also marked the beginning of intense surveillance and scrutinization of John Trudell by the F.B.I. (Federal Bureau of Investigation). Trudell is the proud subject of a 17,000 page FBI file.

The war on America came at great personal, and unimaginable, cost to Trudell.

He was born in Omaha, Nebraska February 15, 1946 growing up on the nearby Santee Sioux reservation. The loss of his mother at an early age and the hardship of watching his father struggle to support their large family cemented in him the economic injustice of the American dream. After a brief stint in the Navy, his disillusionment with the government and justice system, inspired the exploration of indigenous roots.

In a defining moment in February 1979, Trudell burned the flag at a demonstration in Washington, D.C. in front of the J. Edgar Hoover building, the headquarters of the FBI, citing "injustice and racism and classism," as the reasons for the desecration. It is less than 24 hours later that his wife, her mother, and their three children were killed in a fire of "suspicious origin" on the Shoshone Paiute reservation in Nevada. How to handle such overwhelming pain? Travel, write, get the message out to as many ears as can stand to listen. Through the heartache which follows him for the 100,000 miles he is to travel in the next 3 years, his spirit begins the process of speaking through poetry, then music - encapsulating his loss - "it was murder, they were murdered as an act of war." he says flatly.

His poetry evolved into a book he published in 1981 called "Living in Reality." The inspiration of friend and musician Jackson Browne opened him to the world of music, eventually forming "The Grafitti Band" with Jesse Ed Davis, a Kiowa, in 1985. The next two releases, "AKA Grafitti Man" and "HeartJump Bouquet" were followed by the death of Jesse Ed in 1988. Other releases followed: "Tribal Voice," "But this Isn't El Salvador," "Child's Voice," and a new remixed version of "AKA Grafitti Man."

What more can such a visual, vocal activist do? Go west, to Hollywood. Appearing in several movies - Michael Apted's "Incident at Oglala," "Thunderheart," and Steven Segal's "On Deadly Ground," raised Trudells name and face to international recognition.

"He was an inspiration to me in making the documentary film "Incident at Oglala" about Leonard Peltier's fight for justice," says Director Apted, "so much that I cast him as the charismatic Indian leader in "Thunderheart" a movie that deals with the government oppression of the contemporary native American. There wasn't an untruthful moment in his performance."

"Sometimes they have to kill us," he told me, "because they cannot break our spirit." John is one of those rare unbreakable spirits."

The release of his second book "Stickman" in 1994 raised him to another level of visibility in the media.

"Crazy Horse didn't want his picture taken because he didn't want it to capture his spirit. Me, I'm gonna use my picture to carry mine." he says.

Trudell now seems more hopeful than he has in years, he is being seen not just as a poet, or musician, or actor but as a complex American figure - engaging, enigmatic and slightly dangerous. He won Artist of the Year at the 1999 Nammys for his album "Blue Indians" produced by folk singer Jackson Browne.

"John Trudell is a crazy lone wolf, poet, prophet, preacher, warrior full of pain and fun and laughter and love… He is a reality check. Justice is a fire that burns inside him. His spirit cries out for it. It makes him dangerous." says Kris Kristofferson

One of the more intense groups at the concert was Ulali which features Pura Fe (Tuscarora), Soni Primo (Apache/Mayan) and Jennifer Kreiger (Tuscarora).

These three native women a cappella singers deliver a mystical and sweeping sound that evolves from blending a variety of traditional and contemporary indigenous music of the Americas. American audiences got their first taste of Ulali when they appeared on the soundtrack to Turner documentary series, "The Native Americans", and subsequently had two of their songs, including the contemporary "Mahk Jchi", featured on the album, "Robbie Robertson and The Red Road Ensemble".

Ulali made their national television debut when they performed on the "Tonight Show with Jay Leno". Singing about the Native struggle and prophecies in a variety of Native languages, the work of Ulali is a form of personal and historic expression. As an early, progressive, and daring Native Women's singing group, Ulali were formerly known under the name of one of its members "Pure Fe".

Pura Fe, was raised in Manhattan, as a classic R&B blues lounge singer who dresses in traditional clothing. She has collaborated on many other Native recordings as well as releasing her own album in 1995 "Caution To The Wind" (Shanachie)

This seven member group then became an a cappella Women's Trio. Ulali can be heard on dozens of albums, documentaries, movies and their award-winning videos, including "Follow Your Heart's Desire" which won Best Music Video at the American Indian Film Festival. The group has been seen on VH-1, CNN, MTV, PBS and Much Music. In 1994, Pura Fe and the group Kanatanaski were Juno Award nominees in the Global Music category for "The Condor Meets The Eagle", a collaborative effort featuring indigenous music from North and South America's. Together with Ulali, they performed as special guests for the Juno Award Ceremonies.

Ulali kicked off the "Honor The Earth Tour" opening for the Indigo Girls for several dates of their national tour in the late 1990s. They have shared the bill with Buffy Saint Marie, Joy Harjo, Holly

From Kokopellis to Electric Warriors
The Native American Culture of Music

Near, Richie Havens, The B-52's, Jackson Browne, Roseanne Cash, Mary Chapin Carpenter, and David Byrne, and collaborated with such artist as Rita Coolidge, Robert Mirabal, JohnTrudell, Gary Farmer, Floyd Westerman, and the Silver Cloud Singers. Other projects include: Smithsonian Folkways compilation CD "Heartbeat", which featured over 30 First Nation Women singers, and supporting music festival. Ulali continues to tour and record internationally.

Sandra Hale Schulman

Bill Miller

From Kokopellis to Electric Warriors
The Native American Culture of Music

Chapter Eight

Into The Mainstream: NAMA

In the early 1990s', a story on Florida band Tiger Tiger's latest album "Dream Scout" was submitted to Billboard magazine as part of their bi-monthly column on the best unsigned talent in America. Several weeks went by and the story never ran. When the editor was asked why, they replied that they didn't think it was something that any mainstream record labels would be interested in.

A year later Billboard published their first Spotlight issue - a special section devoted to just one subject - Native American Music. This nine page feature covered the big picture of the genre - while singling out the eight independent Native American music labels as well as the mainstream labels - Mercury, Warner Brothers, Capitol- that were picking up Native American artists. The special section has run annually ever since.

Sandra Hale Schulman

It quoted artists like Joanelle Nadine Romero who stressed that "It's been difficult to find places where we can perform and be judged simply on the merits of our work. Since Native Music now includes so many different styles and sounds, the need to break out of the reservation is more important than ever."

"Part of the process is educating our own people," admitted Tom Bee, president of SOAR Records. "We strive to book our contemporary artists at traditional Indian gatherings so people can see and hear for themselves what's happening in their musical culture. It's the first step toward the mainstream."

Legitimizing Native American Music as a format is the current goal of marketing and public relations visionary Ellen Bello. She is based in a New York City office on the aptly named Avenue of the Americas, where sage burns next to computers and stacks of CDs and magazines. Bello is almost single handedly taking Native American music to the masses.

As the founder of In-Press Communications - a national public relations, management and marketing firm that specialized in recording artists, In-Press became the first firm to represent Native

American artists Robbie Robertson, Rita Coolidge & Walela, Mirabal, Songcatchers, Burning Sky, Pura Fe and Red Thunder.

Bello was responsible for securing performances for her artists at the 1996 Olympic Games in Atlanta Georgia, the Democratic National Convention and at Presidential Inaugural Balls. She has served as a judge at the Gathering Of Nations and has contributed to the New York weekly The Village Voice. She has no Indian heritage, but her spirit is as strong as a full-blood.

"This is a genre that just won't let me go," says Bello. "When I first heard this music I was blown away by the heart and struggle of it. The key to all this is creating the same things that other formats have, like weekly charts (collected from radio stations across the country), a website, an association (the Native American Music Association, formed in 1996) and an awards show."

A chart from March 25, 1999 listed the following top ten albums as compiled by the playlists of stations in Wisconsin, Alaska, Colorado, Arizona and Montana:

1. Ghost Dance Bill Miller (SOL Records)

2. Enter The Circle Black Lodge Singers (Canyon)

3. Alligator Tales Chief Jim Billie (SOAR)

4. Things We Do Indigenous (Pachyderm)

5. Peyote Songs Primeau & Mike (Canyon)

6. Contact From The Underworld Of Redboy Robbie Robertson (Capitol)

7. Stoney Park Schemitzun Stoney Park (Sweetgrass)

8. Spirit Nation Spirit Nation (V2 Records)

9. It's Time To Round Dance Northern Cree Singers (Canyon)

10. A Native American Odyssey Various Artists (Putamayo)

The charts have been running in publications such as Indian News Newspaper and Native Voices Magazine.

Bello's biggest event was five years in the making, a show planned to honor Native American artists that until 2000 did not even get a category in the Grammys. After the major success of the second show, the National Academy of Recording Arts and Sciences -the Grammy people and their president Michael Greene - called Bello and asked for a proposal to create a new category for the Grammys. The new category was officially added on June 6th, 2000 for the award show in 2001. Previously Native American music had been placed in the Folk, World or New Age categories.

"Just a few years ago, the number of artists, releases and industry support necessary to create a category for Native American Music did not exist," said Greene. "The face of music is changing and growing. Different cultures which rarely received much public attention are beginning to be recognized. Our understanding of the music, traditions and challenges which face this community are growing. The Academy is pleased to be able to acknowledge the achievements of these musical styles with a new category."

To their credit, NARAS had been working in the Native American community conducting educational and cultural programs in Santa Fe and Oklahoma City.

Small bumps in that red road included requests to NARAS that only Federally recognized artists be eligible for the award nomination. After some discussion and research, Bello realized that the Grammys make no such concession for any other category and neither NAMA or the Grammy organization NARAS use federal funds, so NAMA was under no obligation to have that credential. It would have been "an administrative and political nightmare" said NARAS.

A thorough screening committee has been established to make sure any submitted work is serious and artistic in nature, so the chances of a non-native being nominated are eliminated. The Native American Music Awards contain a category called Native Heart that allows for work by non-natives to be recognized, but it's unlikely such a category will ever be in the Grammy awards.

The first Native American Music Awards show was held on May 24, 1998 at the enormously successful Foxwoods Resort Casino in Connecticut, which is owned by the Pequot tribe. The show served as a who's who in Native America and played a major role in educating the public about Native Americans in the arts - people that range from Jimi Hendrix to Elvis Presley, James Dean, Willie Nelson and ebullient host Wayne Newton.

Presenters included Joe Walsh, Bruce Cockburn, Richie Havens and John Trudell. Live performances were interspersed with 20 award presentations, plus a Lifetime Achievement Award for Robbie

From Kokopellis to Electric Warriors
The Native American Culture of Music

Robertson's tireless efforts in both music and the Native American rights struggle.

The success of the event led to international press coverage, plans for a compilation CD of the winners and an international tour. The event was filmed and broadcast on the A&E channel. Bello also has begun compiling an archive of music and a TV show to highlight Native American dance. NAMA's website (www.nativeamericanmusic.com) got 10,000 hits the first month, just a small indication of the potential audience.

"Native American Music has taken a giant step forward with these shows," says Bello. "The time is right for this music and these artists to find their rightful place in the mainstream."

By the second NAMA show in November 1999, the award categories had doubled to include the far reaching genres of rap/hip hop, blues/jazz and folk/country.

"Since last years show, the number of recordings up for nomination is 144, double the previous year," says Bello. "Why this incredible leap? The recognition at the last ceremony may have inspired artists, and there needs to be a supporting network beneath us to get those recordings out. Whether it's Canyon or Silverwave (record companies), the distributors are doubling their efforts. It's important to see this as it's own industry."

New Mexico was a fitting place to stage the second award show. Deep in the heart of Indian country, the symbol of the state depicts the four winds, the four seasons, the four times of day and the four stages of life. Everything has a spirit here, a philosophy that was taught as far back as the original inhabitants of the southwest, the Anasazi.

The day before the second NAMA show in Albuquerque, Bill Miller was seeing spirits and having visions. His band members eyed him warily as the stone cold sober Miller seemed to be off in a world of his own, eyes wide and hallucinating. Hours later he recalled seeing vast windy canyons and vibrant blooming roses.

"They were as real as anything," a slightly dazed Miller says. "I get this from time to time, I always hope it's important."

The next night a visibly shaken, tearful Miller won five awards including Artist of the Year, Song of the Year and Best Male Artist. During his heartfelt acceptance speeches he thanked his wife, children, band members and particularly his father, who died of alcoholism five years earlier. Miller's riveting performance of "Ghost Dance" drew a standing ovation, although he later said the song almost didn't get recorded as it was written as a private remembrance. Miller is emerging as a top notch American performer after several years of touring, writing and releasing several albums.

"To be with this many Indian people being proud of being Indian is great," Miller said. "There's nothing like it. If we have to have the party ourselves, we will," he said.

"It was crackling in there!" exclaimed Arigon Starr who won the Best Independent Recording category and also performed. "There was so much electricity in that room. It's the best audience we've ever played to."

Presenter Rodney Grant of "Dances With Wolves" proclaimed, "There are no losers here tonight. It's a great night to be Indigenous, isn't it?"

First winner of the evening, P.M. Begay leaped to her feet when her name was announced, hugged her friends, clapped, jumped up and down, then sat back down. Suddenly, she realized the audience was waiting for her to go to the stage to receive her award. She did.

Younger brothers Michael and Samuel Begay presented her the award for Best Children's Recording, "To All Our Precious Ones."

Best Female Artist JoAnne Shenandoah thanked "all those who have gone before us - our grandmothers who kept the songs, those who gave us beautiful music to give the world."

The next generation of Native American stars made themselves heard loud and clear during the show, as New York City resident Wayquay rocked the house with her stylized brand of rock, dance and native chants.

A stunning almond eyed beauty, Swangideed Wayquay, of Ojibway Anishnabe heritage, produced a video from her CD "Tribal Grind" that has already won awards at the American Indian Film Festival and took top honors this year at the Native American Music Awards.

No stranger to the spotlight, Wayquay has appeared on CNN Worldbeat, CNN Showbiz, Good Morning Live and on TV in Montreal. A whirlwind of energy, Wayquay's throaty laugh and unabashed candor ("You should see that size of the rats in my neighborhood!" she shrieks) have endeared her to media and fans alike. In contrast to the subdued, reverential style of Joanne Shenandoah, Wayquay comes on like a wild eyed leopard, tossing her waist length black hair and chanting like a banshee under a full moon. She wears black leather pants under long crocheted dresses and dances in elegant circles while stomping her city tough boots.

Another unusual performer turned up at the show for the Hall of Fame tribute to Hank Williams Sr. - his wild child grandson Shelton Hank Williams III, who claims Indian heritage of Cree and Cherokee on both sides of his famous grandparents.

A youthful 29, Hank III has the same pale, gaunt build as granddad, along with a slightly dangerous, dog-eared edge. Everyday attire is slightly rumpled western shirts emblazoned with roses, dice and flames; a beat to hell cream colored cowboy hat, baggy black jeans and pointy two toned boots held together with "hillbilly chrome" - silver duct tape. His pitch perfect yodel and desolate song imagery conjure up endless miles of road, long lonesome nights and the godawful feel that nowhere is home.

In Shelton's teen years he played in punk bands, did a lot of drugs and idolized the late rocker Sid Vicious. "I think my Mom got kinda freaked out by the whole thing," he says quietly.

In 1996 Shelton got served paternity papers while onstage during a gig from a one night stand he had when he was 17. It was time to pay the future piper by looking to the past. He played shows in Branson Missouri doing nothing but Hank Sr. covers and recorded an album called "Three Hanks: Men With Broken Hearts" with his father that digitally harmonized all three generations of Williams's. The look and the sound was unmistakable. The torch it seems, had been passed by skipping a generation - since his dad Hank Jr. has long been a caricature of the southern white trash rebel.

"Of course I never met him," Shelton says of his legendary grandfather who died 20 years before he was born. "But like everyone else I know him through his music. My dad doesn't even talk about him much. We're not that close and there'll always be some weirdness there."

Shelton lives in a beat up house in East Nashville with four other guys, his car is a late 60s model Cadillac that sports a license plate reading the same as his tattoo "Risin Outlaw". He has seen none of granddads, or dads money, and it's doubtful he will for years.

"Well, it's their money, not mine," he shrugs.

When in Nashville he plays at Lower Broadway honky tonks like the Bluegrass Inn and rocks out at hard core punk shows. He sleeps 'til five in the afternoon most days and has given his label - Curb Records - hell for the way they've handled his record. But the press has been Shelton's biggest ally - full feature stories in Rolling Stone, the Los Angeles Times and GQ magazine have propelled his famous name and razor sharp face into the stratosphere.

Three straight weeks in a rundown turquoise colored bus with seven other guys had left Shelton in a pissy mood. The band had been on the road promoting Hank's debut CD "Risin' Outlaw" which had been garnering rave reviews from the New York Post, and had hit the top ten Americana chart within a week. But Hank was blasting the album at every turn, calling the label Communists and claiming it didn't represent what he was about.

Shelton's first stop in Albuquerque was an infamous Route 66 tattoo parlor, where he spent four hours getting a bright red devil bird inked into his left forearm. "Maybe it's too bright," he muttered as the arm swelled and oozed hours later.

But the show performance pulled everything together as the audience, most of whom had never heard of him before, hooted and stomped along to the honky tonk strains of "Move It On Over". The song was the tribute performance as Hank Williams Sr. was inducted into the Native American Music Awards Hall of Fame.

At the after show party, dozens lined up for autographs as photographers pushed Shelton and Houston Geronimo, the great, great grandson of Chief Geronimo, together for a modern day Cowboys and Indians portrait.

But Shelton was more interested in meeting drummer Randy Castillo, a half Indian, half Spanish heavy metal drummer for Motley Crue and Ozzy Osbourne; and John Densmore of The Doors, whose lead singer Jim Morrison claimed to have been inhabited by Indian spirits and died young in a Paris bathtub of an overdose. For generations of musical geniuses, old habits die hard.

As this book was going to print in April 2002 we received the sad word that Randy Castillo died of cancer at age 51 in Los Angeles. At the time he was putting a new band together and was producing an album of Native/Latin music. We'll miss you Randy, vaya con dios.

This show also saw the reunion of rock band XIT, the group founded in 1969 by Tom Bee that was said to be "too radical" at it's inception. They released an album in 1971 "Plight of the Redman" and toured worldwide. This reunion found them playing together for the first time in almost 20 years. One original member is Jim Boyd, who was with the band from 1978 to 1982, and went on to compose the award winning Smoke Signals soundtrack with Sherman Alexie.

NAMA also added special sports awards this year, named after athlete Jim Thorpe, and continued giving thousands of dollars in scholarships to deserving students.

The after party at a nearby hotel raged on well past midnight with the performers mingling with the guests and fans. Flashbulbs popped, autographs were begged for and the buffet line stretched out the door. Actor Wes Studi cornered Rita Coolidge for some LA movie talk, Rodney Grant strutted around in a top hat, Bill Miller gave countless interviews.

The award show will be produced in Albuquerque for 2000 and 2001. Then for NAMA's five year anniversary in 2002 the award show will be held at the Indian Summer Festival in Milwaukee with an audience of 10,000 expected, and a Best of Nammy's Show is planned to take back the island of Manhattan, an old Indian stomping ground.

"It's really been growing at an amazing rate," says Bello. "the time was just right to pool all these resources to create something unified."

NAMA Proposal To NARAS For A Grammy Category

(This proposal was submitted in early 2000, the category was officially instated June 6, 2000)

"The music and the business of Native American culture is sometimes hard to get a handle on. Yet no matter what the vantage point; one aspect of this multi-faceted musical world is obvious; it is big and getting bigger"—Davin Seay, Billboard Magazine

One of the main objectives of the Native American Music Association is to continue developing and presenting contemporary Native music as a popular music genre of growing national interest. Therefore, on behalf of our entire membership, and the nation's American Indian and music communities, please accept the following as a proposal for N.A.R.A.S. to consider creating a collaborative program with our organization/or establishing a Grammy Award category that honors recordings containing Native American music components to help us achieve our objective.

I. MODERN DEFINITION OF NATIVE AMERICAN MUSIC

When Native American music was originally born outdoors it used scales and tones unlike that of the Western World. The early fieldwork of scholars, anthropologists, ethnomusicologists and others on traditional music proved that it was just as emotional, complex and cultivated as any other modern art form. Ethnomusicologist, Natalie Curtis recognized the uniqueness of Native Americans and the value of their art. She found their music to be, "exciting, exhilarating, and inspiring through its spirit and vitality". She called them "a people of real creative artistic genius" and "artistic by nature... His art is the unconscious striving of the many to make beautiful the things of daily living." She felt the music of the Native American presented material absolutely unique and believed it should be of interest and value to the whole human race."

Anthropologist Alice Fletcher noticed that this music possessed "a charm of spontaneity that cannot fail to please those who would come near to nature and enjoy the expression of emotion untrammeled by the intellectual control of schools." Traditional Native music also preserved history, and the songs of a tribe served as its heritage. Care was taken to transmit songs accurately, from generation to generation, without external aids of a written language. Fletcher also learned that Indian songs traveled far; those of one tribe were soon another. But tribes always credited other tribes to whom the songs belonged. Fletcher never met an instance of plagiarism and learned that certain kinds of songs could be purchased by individuals. If a song became personal property through such a purchase, the purchaser would never claim to have composed it; thus showing that Native American culture even possessed a sense of the music business as we know it today.

Contemporary Native American music resists simple categorization and reflects various musical influences and cultural traditions. Today, Native American music has taken more of the lines of America's artistic forms. Although it encompasses the past, particular traditions have come to an end or have been modified. One thing remains certain; we are all experiencing a very exciting time of documented change in the folklife of the American Indian.

Through the eyes four contemporary artists, we can easily determine which traditional aspects are being incorporated and how such usage is determined. Artists like Robert Mirabal skillfully merges his ancient Taos Pueblo culture with that of modern contemporary rock music; Joanne Shenandoah ingeniously rearranges melodies, rhythm and lyric variations on traditional Iroquois themes into a contemporary folk format; Rita Coolidge and Walela's music was born out of a vision and a promise to their grandmother to keep her stories alive; and Grammy nominee, R. Carlos Nakai's use of the flute reminds us of the history of his ancestors in Canyon de Chelly.

Sandra Hale Schulman

From a music that was born outdoors with high-pitched vocals and nature sounds, most contemporary artists compensate the lost nature world with modern instrumentation and technology. Their traditional perspectives and values are being reaffirmed through their current musical works.

From the flute and drum to chants and ambient soundscapes, Native American music carries a deep reverence of America's landscapes where songs symbolize the unification of a global family; of all races and colors, the wisdom of the elders, and the spirit and beauty of nature that we live among. A consistently distinct element of today's Native American music is the usage of vocables or vocals performed in tribal language and/or the utilization of natural instrumentation such as; hand-made drums, rattles, gourds, bells and flutes. There are some instances of Native American artists performing and creating popular music without containing any of these bases. However, they may reflect their Native American identity or the Native American experience through their lyrical content. Today, most artists who attempt to "recreate" Native American music now work from a traditional base but within a contemporary sensibility; using modern recording techniques and blending traditional and contemporary instruments and arrangements. The flute remains a consistent instrument in these music initiatives as does the drum.

New initiatives also tend to recreate natural sounds from the environment; running water, thunder, wind, etc. Two elements are certain: 1) As with its traditional origins, the primary role of Native American song should offer elements that heal, inspire positive feelings and joyous occasions, and 2) The result of today's contemporary Native American music ultimately retains its' cultural identity.

II. MARKET OVERVIEW

A. National Retail Chains Carrying Native American Music Recordings:

Barnes & Noble

Borders

HMV

Musicland

> Tower Records
>
> Virgin Mega Store

B. Reported Increase in National Retail Sales Per Year

   In a Billboard cover story, "Native American Music Rising" (November 27, 1999), local Hastings outlets in New Mexico sited a sales increase of 83% and a world music buyer for Tower Records in Denver sited a "quadrupling" of sales in the past year.

   Border Books & music at the World Trade Center in New York City estimates at 25% increase in their Native American sales and acquisitions in the past year.

   Independent record companies specializing in Native American Music site an increase in sales ranging from 5 - 20% over the past year.

C. In a survey conducted by the Native American Music Association, the overall number of titles released by Native American record companies have:

   - Increased for almost every label
   - Have featured more contemporary genre formats

- Have featured more traditional formats
- Have acquired increased distribution

D. Largest selling Native American Recordings to date:

"Canyon Trilogy," R. Carlos Nakai (Canyon Records 1989) - Gold status

"Walela," Walela (Mercury/Triloka) - Gold status

"Music For The Native Americas," Robbie Robertson & The Red Road Ensemble (Capitol Records 1994) - 1/4 million in sales

"Sacred Spirit" (Virgin 1994) 100,000 US.; over 3 million overseas

"We The People" Brule nearing 500,000 units sold

"Walela" Walela (Triloka 1997) nearing 500,000 units sold

E. E-commerce sites or E-Tailers featuring Native American Music:

Amazon.com - since June 1998

Yahoo Music Shopping

CDNow

Virgin Megastore.com since 1999

F. Commercial Radio Stations that Air Native American Music Recordings:

 KTAO Taos, New Mexico

 KBAC Santa Fe, NM

 KCTY Omaha, NB

 KGSR Austin, TX

 KHUM Humboldt, CA

 KNBA Anchorage, AL

 KPIG Monterey, CA

 KSPN Apsen, CO

 WNCS Montpelier, VT

 WYYB Nashville, TN

G. National Radio Charts That Have Featured Native American Music Recordings:

 Album Network, Gavin & FMQB - Non-comercial Triple A charts

 Bill Miller

 John Trudell

Indigenous

Walela

Robbie Robertson

R&R, Album Network, Gavin & FMQB - Commercial Triple A charts

Robbie Robertson

Indigenous

NAV "Walk Between Worlds," Golana Awo - #2

Billboard World Music Chart

"Kolonaha, From The Gentle Wind," Keda Beamer (Dancing Cat/Windham Hill)

"Hui Aloha," Hui Aloha (Dancing Cat/Windham Hill)

H. National Awards Shows Featuring Native American Music Categories:

NAV (Association For Independent Music) - US

NAMA (Native American Music Awards) - US

Canadian Aboriginal Achievement Awards - Canada

Junos - Canada

First Americans In The Arts - US

Crossroads Magazine - US

I. Average # of National Native American Music Recordings Released Per Year (nationally distributed):

1994 - 1996	55
1997	64
1998	144
1999	98

Note: In 1998, the average figure more than doubled reaching a record- breaking total of national recordings that year.

J. U.S. Record Labels That Have Released Native American Music Recordings In The Past Decade

<u>MAJOR LABELS</u>

A&M/HORIZON ALMO SOUNDS

ANGEL/EMI

BEGGARS BANQUET

CAPITOL CURB

KOCH INTERNATIONAL

MERCURY/TRILOKA

From Kokopellis to Electric Warriors
The Native American Culture of Music

REPRISE RYKODISC

SHANACHIE

SONY WORK

SONY/TRISTAR

EPIC

TVT V2

VIRGIN

WARNER BROS.

WARNER WESTERN

WINDHAM HILL

SPECIALTY & INDEPENDENT LABELS

BIG MOUTH

BLACKMOON

BLUE JACKELL

CACHET

CANYON

CARIBOU

CELESTIAL HARMONIES

COOL RUNNINGS

DAEMON

DANCING CAT

DRUM BEAT& INDIAN ARTS

EARTHBEAT/MUSIC FOR LITTLE PEOPLE

EARTHSEA

GLOBAL BEAT

GREEN LINNETT RECORDS

HELICON RECORDS

HEARTS OF SPACE

INTUITIVE

IRIE CULTURE

LAUGHING CAT

LISTENING LIBRARY

MAKOCHE

MUSIC OF THE WORLD

NATURAL VISIONS

NEW WORLD

OGINALI

From Kokopellis to Electric Warriors
The Native American Culture of Music

OREADE/BLUESTAR

PACHYDERM

PUTUMAYO

RED FEATHER

RED REVEREND

RED VINYL

ROCK POWER

SILVER WAVE

SMITHSONIAN FOLKWAYS

SOAR

SOL

SUNSHINE

SWEETGRASS

TACAHO PRODUCTIONS

TALKING TACO

TATANKA RECORDS

THUNDERWOLF

TRILOKA

TURTLE ISLAND

WACKY

WITHOUT REZ

K. Recording artists with multiple releases that have been archived by the Native American Music Association over the past ten years:

<u>ARTISTS</u>

Alph Secakuku (2)

Arigon Starr (2)

Bill Miller (3)

Blacklodge Singers (4)

Brule (3)

Burning Sky (4)

Chief Jim Billie (2)

Coyote Oldman (2)

Indigenous (4)

J. Hubert Francis (2)

Jack Gladstone (5)

Jana (2)

Jay Begaye (2)

From Kokopellis to Electric Warriors
The Native American Culture of Music

Jerry Alfred (2)

Jim Beer (2)

Joanne Shenandoah (9)

John Trudell (3)

Kashtin (3)

Kevin Locke (3)

Lee & Stephen Tiger (2)

Litefoot (3)

Little Wolf/Jim Wilson (2)

Mary Youngblood (2)

Mocassin Flats (2)

Northern Cree Singers (3)

Peacemaker (2)

Peter Kater & R. Carlos Nakai (4)

Primeaux & Mike (4)

R. Carlos Nakai (7)

Red Bull (3)

Robbie Robertson (2)

Robert Mirabal (4)

Robert Tree Cody (2)

Sharon Burch (2)

Songcatchers (2)

Tsa'ne Do'se (2)

Walela (2)

Without Reservation (2)

XIT (5)

Young Grey Horse (2)

From Kokopellis to Electric Warriors
The Native American Culture of Music

Bill Miller, Hank III, Randy Castillo, backstage at the 1999 Nammys

XIT Photo by: Kimberlie R. Hall

Sandra Hale Schulman

Rodney Grant, NAMA 1999

From Kokopellis to Electric Warriors
The Native American Culture of Music

Wayquay, Ellen Bello, Joanne Shenandoah at the Nammys 1999

Sandra Hale Schulman

Hank Williams III

Chapter Nine

The Festivals

Honor The Earth Music Tours

One of the most ambitious projects to bring Native American music and environmental problems into the mainstream is the Honor The Earth Music CD and tours. Since 1993, Honor the Earth has sponsored three concert tours featuring the Grammy Award winning Indigo Girls and a host of Native musicians, including Indigenous, Ulali, John Trudell and Keith Secola and the Wild Band of Indians.

A two disc CD was released in 1996 by Daemon and spearheaded by the Indigo Girls. With an impressive roster of artists - Bonnie Raitt, Soul Asylum, Ulali, Rusted Root and a dozen more, the CD laid out the causes and environmental concerns that it stands for.

The tours have collectively raised over half a million dollars that was distributed to 65 Native groups. The tours also raised significant political resources for Native environmentalism, including local and national media coverage and prominent internet exposure. Live broadcasts with activists at the shows allowed Native peoples to report on their own struggles to a world-wide audience.

The Honor the Earth Tours also allowed music fans the opportunity to take action in solidarity with Native peoples. Fans signed more than 100, political "action cards" that were sent to key decision-makers on issues ranging from nuclear waste storage to the Yellowstone buffalo slaughter.

From the Honor The earth website:

"Our first tour in 1993 included stops in three midwest cities. Because of the success and impact of this small tour, the Indigo Girls decided to devote a month of their time in 1995 and again, in 1997 to Honor the Earth. We sponsored a precedent setting 21-stop tour both years. These month long tours combined shows in towns and cities along our route with visits to Native communities."

A letter from the Indigo Girls describes the artists of Honor the Earth tour experience, stating, "this journey had a profound impact on our lives and challenged us to re-examine our own approach to environmental issues."

From Kokopellis to Electric Warriors
The Native American Culture of Music

©Honor the Earth, PO Box 75423, St. Paul, MN 55175

phone 1.800.earth.07 / fax 612.721.1918 /

honorearth@earthlink.net

Native American Blues Festival

The Native American Music Association (NAMA) has started a series of annual Native American Blues Festivals, produced by Donald Kelly, celebrating and showcasing the diverse cultures of Native America. The Festivals feature leading and award winning contemporary artists along with traditional Native American arts and crafts.

The First Native American Blues festival was held at the Tribeca Blues Club in New York City in May 2001. The festival received high critical acclaim and was covered by every New York major newspaper from the *New York Times to the Daily News and Village Voice.*

The Second Annual Native American Blues Festival was a special one day outdoor festival in May 2002 that featured contemporary

Native American blues bands and was held at the Soboba Casino Amphitheater in San Jacinto, California.

Hosted by actor Rodney Grant, (Dances With Wolves), the show featured musical guests Keith Secola & Wild Band of Indians with special guest John Densmore (The Doors), Jim Boyd, Greg Serrato, Tracy Nelson & Native Blues Band, Redman Blues Band, and Arigon Starr. The Native American Blues Festival was a great family outing for both the Native and non-Native communities.

"It's the Blues Music that always moved me," says producer Donald Kelly. "Listening to guy's like Jimmy Wolf and Keith Secola add a Native American twist to the blues compelled me to pursue an outlet to showcase the many talented Native American Blues Musicians out there. Each year the number of Native Blues Bands continues to increase and they are always willing to do what it takes to make this event happen. Call me selfish but I just love the blues and every year it keeps growing. We will triple our attendance from last year and the reception from the Native Community is always with open arms."

Kelly is also a producer with The Native American Music Association, a non-profit organization, which preserves and promotes the rich oral history and heritage of Native America. The Association has presented four annual sold-out Native American Music Awards (NAMMYS) shows, two annual festivals, provided Native youth with scholarships, seminars, and professional training, assisted in the creation of a Native music category in the Grammys, and established the nations largest Native American music archive. Contact www.nativeamericanmusic.com. (For more on NAMA see Chapter 9)

Native American Music Festival

Established in 1999 by the Shakopee Mdewakanton Sioux Community in Minnesota, the first years show was a sold out performance of music by Buffy St. Marie, blues rockers Indigenous, dance music innovator Brule, actor/rapper Litefot, the gorgeous harmonies of Ulali, and new comer Derek Miller whose influences range from blues, rock and folk. Miller has already won three awards from the Canadian Aboriginal Music Awards. For information on future festivals call 952-496-6160.

Sandra Hale Schulman

Native American Performing Arts Festival:

Native Roots And Rhythms

Featuring contemporary and traditional Indigenous performers, this annual event is a major festival in Santa Fe, New Mexico.

Usually taking place in August, the Festival features music, dance, storytelling, comedy and film.

Artists who have appeared include Bill Miller, Robert Mirabal, Star Nayea, Matthew Andrae, Kevin Locke, Jerry Alfred, Rulan Tangen, NR&R Dance Ensemble and singers and dancers from 19 pueblos.

Information call 505-989-8898.

Indian Summer Festival

This year's Annual Indian Summer Festival will be held as usual in Sept. (2002 date is Sept. 6-8th) at Milwaukee's beautiful lakefront Henry Maier Festival Park and celebrates the theme "Coming Home." Tickets are available by sending a self-addressed stamped envelope

From Kokopellis to Electric Warriors
The Native American Culture of Music

with a check or money, to the Indian Summer Office, 7441 W. Greenfield Ave., Suite 109, Milwaukee, WI 53214. Office hours are 9am - 3 pm.

An annual poster contest is held to select a poster which best depicts the festival theme. The entries are displayed and a festival poster is selected at the Winter Pow Wow.

The great variety of events, entertainment, demonstrations and hands-on activities mean there's something for everyone at the nation's largest American Indian cultural festival. Families appreciate the fact that since festival areas where cultural activities occur are blessed and thus considered sacred, alcoholic beverages are allowed only in the areas around contemporary music stages.

When all this activity whets appetites, festival attendees can sample some American Indian favorites such as Indian fry bread, Indian tacos and buffalo burgers.

The festival's competition Pow Wow awards $35,000, and amazes with its glorious mix of sights and sounds. During special "intertribal" dances, audience members are invited to watch or join in the Pow

Sandra Hale Schulman

Wow and do not need to be American Indian or wear a dance outfit to participate.

Cultural performers add to the uniqueness of the festival, along with hoop and social dancing, magic and more. Visitors to the festival can watch people from many different American Indian nations demonstrate traditional skills that were, in many cases, learned from parents or grandparents.

Families can watch and ask questions as artisans do quill work, make moccasins, demonstrate basket-making, explain finger-weaving, carve totem poles and effigies, weave blankets, and create pine needle art.

On the festival's music stages, contemporary American Indian performers cover tastes from country to blues to jazz to rock. Nationally known entertainers such as Douglas Spotted Eagle, Brule', and Star Nayea have become Indian Summer "regulars" who draw their fans to the festival and make new ones.

Indian Summer's villages, where traditional dwellings are recreated, bring to life time-honored traditions. The birch bark wigwams and wooden lodges of the Woodland Nations stand next to the teepees of the Plains Indians. Nearby, a rustic encampment captures the daily life of the traders and settlers that lived and worked with American Indians.

Demonstrations and games bring the exciting action of the original American Indian sport, lacrosse, to the festival. At the Indian Summer sports area, volunteers from the audience are given hands-on instruction in this centuries old game.

The environmental area focuses on preserving the earth and its creatures. Special displays and entertainers provide an opportunity to understand and appreciate wild living things and the importance of preserving the world in which they live.

The Circle of Fine Art Exhibition displays fine art with American Indian themes. Many of the country's best-known Native American artists display works for viewing and for purchase.

In the vendor marketplace, over 70 merchants from all over the country offer an array of crafts, toys, jewelry, music recordings, clothing, publications and other merchandise. This is truly kid-friendly shopping, where just a few dollars can purchase an animal skin, wooden flute, or child-size ring.

Fireworks at 10:00 PM on Friday and Saturday.

Sponsored by Potawatomi Bingo Casino. Again this year during the fireworks, they will have the dramatic torch-lit canoe procession.

On Sunday, there is a non-denominational Prayer Ceremony at 10 a.m. in the Marcus Amphitheater. The ceremony is opened with the traditional blessing and burning of sweet grass, and includes American Indian singing and drumming. Those attending gain free entry to the festival after the prayer ceremony at approximately noon.

From Kokopellis to Electric Warriors
The Native American Culture of Music

Chapter Ten

Mr. Las Vegas: Wayne Newton

Las Vegas Nevada is still Wayne Newton's town. One of the most successful Native American performers of the 20th century, Wayne Newton personifies the glitz, schmaltz and unabashed showmanship of nightclub performers.

But he never fails to mention his Indian heritage - he is half Cherokee and half Powhatan - they are the first words that come out of his mouth in his new show at the Wayne Newton Theater at the Stardust Hotel in Las Vegas. A show for which he is being paid a record 25 million dollars for 40 weeks of work a year.

Opening day of the new show on January 24th, 2000, Newton pulled up in a $360,000 Rolls Royce led by a police escort. He then flipped the switch on his theater's new red neon sign bearing his name. He is a big man in a town that has never been bigger.

"I am thrilled to begin what I believe will be the most exciting, productive and fulfilling time of my professional life," Newton said as he lit up the huge $2.5 million dollar sign. Billboards and posters plastered the town, announcing the new deal, his handsome smiling face as bright as the diamond studded watch on his wrist.

The new show is much like some of his previous shows, with Newton covering songs by his "friends" Elvis Presley (another performer with native blood), Bobby Darin, Willie Nelson and Tom Jones. He kisses the women, teases the men, trades jokes with his band members ("This guy here is half Indian and half Jewish. We call him a Shmohawk") and produces a storm of smoke, lightning and curtains of rain for the big finale of "MacArthur Park". The audience the night I saw the show - which included a big convention of American Corn Growers (but we call it Maize) - gave him two standing ovations.

Newton has recorded over 140 albums, had a number one hit with "Danke Schoen," regularly turns up on TV shows and with bit parts in movies. He has won the Congressional Medal of Honor Society's

Distinguished Citizens Award and the American Legend Award. He works tirelessly with children's charities.

He seems genuinely happy on stage, laughing and joking and singing till he's almost hoarse. When Newton hosted the First Annual Native American Awards Show in 1998, his enthusiasm overwhelmed even the shows producers. He even pleaded to be allowed to host the following year.

Starting in the business at age 6, Newton appeared on a daily radio show in the wee hours before he went to school, and begged his way onto traveling Grand Ole Opry shows when they came through his hometown in Virginia. By his late teens he was already playing Vegas six nights a week.

His parents pushed music on him, but refused to discuss his heritage. As Newton told Casino Player magazine "I could not get either of my parents to talk about our heritage. It was almost as if they were ashamed of being Native American. After my dad's passing, one of my uncles gave me a picture of my grandfather in full Indian dress, which I had never seen in my entire life."

A visit to an orphanage in Phoenix Arizona opened Newton's eyes to the number of Indian children there.

"I was so taken with the fact that there were so many tribes represented in that orphanage. A lot of the children were one of a twin, because in those years if an Indian woman had twins, it was believed that they could not have the same father. So they would leave one child on a rock somewhere, or on a doorstep. All these kids were full blooded Native Americans, but they also had very little knowledge of their heritage. I found a kind of kinship with that."

Phoenix was also the first place that Newton was called an "apple" - someone who is red on the outside and white on the inside. That was his turning point, committing him to causes he still works towards.

"My approach to the drinking and drug problems with Native Americans is that you cannot take any people anywhere in the world and make them a ward of the government without anticipating and being inundated with those kinds of problems. Because what you are doing is taking away their pride. You take away their reason for getting up in the morning."

From Kokopellis to Electric Warriors
The Native American Culture of Music

While many Native Americans are against casino gambling in their communities, Newton sees it as the best thing that ever happened to them.

"With the casinos running, the alcohol rate is down, employment is up and it's given a great deal of pride back to a very proud people. Not only are the Native Americans benefiting, but they are being taught how to run their own businesses, and to be competitive in a world in which it is necessary to assimilate."

Newton is now wealthy beyond his wildest dreams, he is married to a beautiful blond woman named Kathleen and lives on a lush and heavily irrigated horse ranch in the ritzy section of a Vegas suburb. But he grew up poor, although he didn't realize it.

"We were poor, but we didn't know it. Our parents went out of their way to do everything they could for us. My dad made about 48 a week, and spent $6 of that on music lessons for my brother and me. And when it looked like we wanted to play ball or do something that all the other kids were doing, my parents simply said 'If you guys don't want to do this, fine. Just tell us. Because if you don't want these lessons we can't afford it. But if you do, we will beg, borrow or steal."

"When I was doing six shows a night as a teen, some one asked me how I could do that. And I said 'Nobody told me it was difficult.'. In many ways my life was more normal than kids who were out on the street."

Newton has always worked and he eventually became famous, but he never was seduced by drugs or drinking. "I was too busy working," he says.

He watched his friend Elvis become so famous he couldn't handle it, and surround himself with people who never had his best interests at heart. He is a big believer in discipline, and not letting minor ups and downs knock him off the track.

"You know being taken advantage of is not such a particularly terrible thing if you learn from it. You get knocked down, there's no crime in that. Not getting up is the crime."

With age has come a humbleness and an urge to help in ways large and small. A current project finds his helping hand extending overseas to Gravesend, England where the remains of 17th Century legend Pocahontas lie. Newton is from the same tribe as her, and was disturbed to hear that her bones were lost when the church in St. Georges gravesite was moved. When the bones are found, Newton plans to build a million dollar memorial for her.

He performed at the annual American Academy of Forensic Sciences to show his appreciation for their work. "He threw in forensics jokes," said one of the members, "everybody loved him."

"I find that the happiest I ever am," he says "is when I can do something unexpected for other people. I'm not looking for any thanks or anything like that, it just gives me great pleasure. It's then that I feel really indulged, like the luckiest guy who ever took a breath of air."

Sandra Hale Schulman

photo by Sandra Schulman

From Kokopellis to Electric Warriors
The Native American Culture of Music

photo by Sandra Schulman

Sandra Hale Schulman

photo by Sandra Schulman

Chapter Eleven

A Journey Home Along The Tourist Trap Trail

I've tried to trace my family roots for years. The trail begins on my mothers side of the family, with the Cherokee name Hale. The road has yielded vague stories from my uncles, trips to Cherokee, North Carolina and Florida and researching Cherokee roll books. I've pored over fading black and white photos of my raven haired, dark eyed relatives, their stiff poses revealing nothing.

I cried the day I stood in a book store and saw the names of my Indian family listed in the Dawes Western Roll book. There were names of the Hales from 150 years ago, some of the same names as my Aunts two generations later.

They must have started in the east - Georgia, Carolina - and walked the Trail of Tears west, only to walk again back east after the Civil War and settle into a life of farming and raising dairy cows.

Sandra Hale Schulman

My mother was born in a small town in Georgia called Thomaston, part of a dry county where all the families were big. They moved often as GrandMama Hale birthed child after child until there were 12. Uncle Paul became a preacher, Uncle Winton a factory worker, Cecil and Floyd soldiers. The beautiful women, my Aunts Mildred and Nellie were happy housewives, birthing several children, never getting an education past high school and never venturing much past the Georgia state lines. Twins were born in the 1920's but died soon after. GrandMama gave birth again in 1932 to my momma Myrtice and her sister Myrtle. They would be the last children. My mother became the best nurse in the world (she won Nursing Director of the Year for a large national nursing home chain), her sister married young and had four children.

While the family was never rich, they were happy and healthy and riotously funny, except for the poor dental health that has plagued the Hale kids all their lives. The women were all tall dark haired beauties, the men lanky and over six feet with cheekbones sharp as knives.

The usual patterns of 20th century families befell them with most marrying young, moving away, going off to war and smoking and eating too much of that fried Southern food.

The most beautiful brother, Cecil, was killed in his early 20's at Iwo Jima, an event that plunged Papa Hale into a silent depression that lasted the rest of his life. Another brother, the wild child Floyd, was the one who brought home monkeys and alligators and cussed like the sailor he became. Years later someone bashed his head in with a rock in New Orleans one night in the early 1960's. Now the multi generations of the family, which numbers in the hundreds, only seems to get together for funerals.

All the "Indianess" is gone, replaced by a Southern Baptist life that was forced on almost all of the Cherokee who lived outside of the reservations. I'm always trying to find it, but much of the trail has gone cold. Still, it's an urge to unearth a story that won't go away, and every little grain of truth I find is a jewel.

Sandra Hale Schulman

Letter from Uncle Paul Hale, St. Petersburg, Fl.:

March 3, 1995

"Our family, so my parents told us, on Papa's side, were born Cherokee. Papa's father, his name was William, his tribe moved East from Oklahoma sometime shortly after the Civil War. They settled in northern Florida, in a small town called Hosford. Some years later, about 1880, they moved to Merriweather County, GA. about two miles from Harris City. Here in 1887 Papa was born. Then his family once again moved back to Hosford when I grew up. He worked on a dairy farm in Savannah, GA. awhile and up in central Georgia where he met Mama. They married in 1913.

Papa's name was Edward Terrell Hale, his brother's name was John Clarence and his sister's name was Minnie. Minnie died rather young, Papa and Uncle John died in the 1960s. Really they both were rather secretive about their family - for some unknown reason. This is why we do not know more of them.

But Cherokee Indian blood does course through all our veins - and the most pronounced Indian features came out in Winton, the oldest brother, Hemon, Uncle John's oldest boy and Mildred, my sister who is dead. Too, in Winton's son Walter (high cheekbones and a somewhat darker complexion). Uncle John's youngest son, Valdez, who killed himself several years ago has a living wife - Sue Hale - who might be able to give you additional information.

This is about all that I know, but believe what I've stated is true. Thank you dear for writing, you and your Mom come visit us when conditions are favorable. Love Paul"

My mother recently wrote a story about her childhood memories that was published in her local Florida newspaper.

"Living in the shadow of the Little White House in Warm Springs, GA is memorable enough, but just think of being a little girl and having F.D.R. stop by your house, spot you on your front porch, stop the motorcade, jump out of his Model T Ford (on crutches), approach you, pat you on the head and say "Hey little girls, how are you?" is an unforgettable experience.

Well this happened to me in 1939. Mr. Roosevelt had just arrived on the train from Washington D.C. enroute to the Little White House for a vacation. People were lined up on the street, waving and screaming. I remember the big and wonderful smile as he waved back at the crowd. He was still smiling when he came to our front porch. After patting me and my twin sister on the head, my momma said "Do you know who that is?" and of course we did not at the age of 7. As he waved goodbye to us, the motorcade sped away to the Little White House.

After that, my fondest memory was having the opportunity to swim in the pool of the warm waters where Roosevelt swam as a treatment for his affliction with polio. He would come to the pool each day to swim with the children also being treated there for polio. The kids had no mercy for him. They ducked him and played water polo with him. On observation, one would never know that any of them had polio.

I never saw him again, but our family had the misfortune of having our brother (21 years of age) get killed in action on Iwo Jima in 1945. The letter arrived at our house giving us the bad news, and yes, FDR had signed the letter. The Purple Heart for bravery arrived shortly afterwards.

From Kokopellis to Electric Warriors
The Native American Culture of Music

I recently revisited the Little White House, saw the Model T Ford on display and the chair he was sitting in posing for a portrait which is unfinished close by. We also went to Pine Mountain where he used to picnic with his family. The fire place is still there. This is a wonderful place to visit and a place in history one should not miss. I'm glad I did not."—Myrtice Hale Bradner

All of this is what has led me to where I am. I remember reading a book when I was about 10, about a beautiful ballerina named Maria Tall Chief, whose long legs and flashing black eyes mesmerized me. I loved dancing and being a tall, dark, slightly gawky kid, she gave me hope.

Growing up in New York City I loved the music clubs - everything from the hard core punk clubs and the music of The Ramones, to the uptown discos where occasional "YMCA Indian chiefs" boogied with the roller bladers; to the Lone Star Cafe on 5th Ave. where I heard country/folk bands like Kinky Friedman and the Texas Jewboys. The only "Indian" things I saw were dusty artifacts in the diaramas at the Museum of Natural History.

Sandra Hale Schulman

Later I moved to Miami, Florida where I became a music writer for a newspaper. I was flooded with CDs every day, some of them from Tiger Tiger and Chief Jim Billie. I went to festivals in the blistering heat of the Everglades to see Redbone and Joanne Shenandoah. The colors and the music and the heat were so intoxicating, I felt I was hallucinating.

I took a trip with my mother to Santa Fe in 1995, riding horses in the Sangre de Christo mountains and hitting the flea markets, pueblos and museums with a vengeance. I loved seeing Mom's happy face at the wonderful Flea Market out in the desert, buying silver earrings by the dozen for her nursing staff. That was a long way from Bloomingdales and Saks Fifth Avenue, where she had taken me to shop from the time I was little.

In January 1995 I wrote a lengthy story for the Fort Lauderdale Sun-Sentinel newspaper called "Music For A Global Tribe" about the emergence of Native American music, both regionally and nationally. That story prompted a phone call from Ellen Bello in New York, who had just begun to put together the Native American Music

Association. She invited me to join them after I left Miami and moved to Nashville.

I hit the ground running with the Association, helping produce segments for the award show, writing stories for the newsletter and CDs NAMA is producing. People as unlikely as Loretta Lynn, her sister Crystal Gayle, and the late punk prince Joey Ramone got involved, before he died he worked with Blackfire - a fierce Navajo punk band out of Arizona.

It's enormously satisfying work, connecting with my roots and making headlines at the same time. The night of the award show in 1999, as the smell of sage hung heavy in the air and the drum circle pounded out rhythms that made my hair stand on end, I stood on the sidelines and wept at the beauty of it.

I know now I've been writing this book all along, in my head and in my heart everytime I heard the music and spent time with the Hale family. I had a cousin Walter, Uncle Winton's son, whose features were more strikingly "Indian" than anyone else in the family. I never got to spend much time with him and he died a few years ago, I regret I never had the chance to ask him what he did in his life.

Sandra Hale Schulman

This road gets more scenic and more interesting every year, it's something that won't let me go. So ultimately that's what this is all about, getting these stories down before they blow away like yesterdays newspapers, like "smoke in the wind" as Walela says.

From Kokopellis to Electric Warriors
The Native American Culture of Music

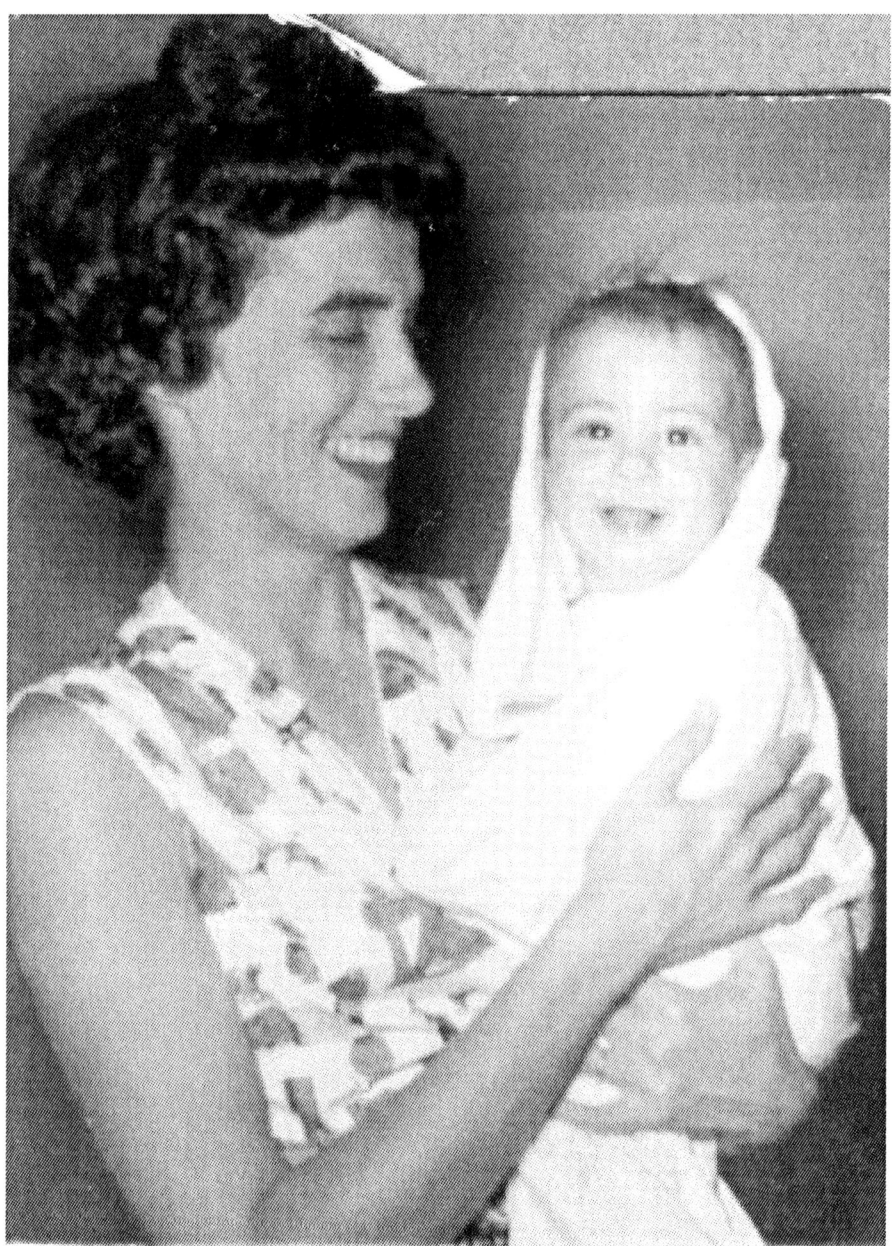

Sandra, Mom – Age 10 months, 1961

My Uncle Cecil Hale with a girlfriend in Georgia 1944, Cecil was killed in Iwo Jima in 1945

From Kokopellis to Electric Warriors
The Native American Culture of Music

Uncle Floyd, my mother Myrtice, Fort Dix, NJ, 1957

Sandra Hale Schulman

Mama, Papa, Stan, 1956

My beautiful mother Myrtice Hale, 1954

Sandra Hale Schulman

About the Author

Sandra Hale Schulman is an entertainment writer, editor and journalist. Her work has appeared in *Billboard, Variety, Country Music Magazine*, and various *Tribune Media* publications. She is on the Board of Directors for the Native American Music Association (NAMA), and is a member of the National Academy of Recording Arts and Sciences (NARAS). Raised in New York, she currently lives in Nashville, Tennessee.

Printed in the United States
44574LVS00006B/346-354